Be refreshed !
Love,
Debbie Furey

Refresh Me with Apples

Debbie Furey

YorkshirePublishing
www.yorkshirepublishing.com
Write Now

Yorkshire Publishing
3207 South Norwood Avenue
Tulsa, OK 74135

ISBN: 978-1-947491-15-1

Table of Contents

Introduction

Song of Solomon 2:3-5 - "Like an apple tree among the trees of the forest is my beloved among the young men. I delight to sit in his shade, and his fruit is sweet to my taste. ⁴ Let him lead me to the banquet hall, and let his banner over me be love. ⁵ Strengthen me with raisins; refresh me with apples, for I am faint with love."

Taking the time to sit down under the shadow of the Lord and partaking of intimate conversation has brought a sweet delight to my morning schedule. It has taught me to wait on the Lord and listen for His still small voice. The words do not come audibly, but slip in unawares, not framed from my thoughts, but appearing as an inner voice or thought telling me something.

Some have asked me, "Where do you get the ideas for these poems"?

It starts with a line of poetry appearing in my mind, and I write it down. It is not until I write it down, that I will get the next line or thought. In some of the poems, I do not even know what the topic will be until the second stanza. Most times, I have a general idea, but always I listen for each line without trying to think of what to write next. Other times I get the thought or the general message and have to compose the line myself and try to think of words that rhyme.

There are times I awake in the middle of the night and get the first line of a poem. I get out of bed right away so I don't lose the inspiration. It is worth losing a few hours of sleep to hear what the Lord might be saying to my spirit.

One thinks of prayers as talking to God, but true conversation is allowing the time to listen to the thoughts of others, as well as making our thoughts known.

The Lord has much to tell us. Listen! Can you hear His arrival? He is standing outside waiting to be let in. Open the door. Invite Him in.

Song of Solomon 2:8, 9 – "Listen! My beloved! Look! Here he comes, leaping across the mountains, bounding over the hills. ⁹ My beloved is like a gazelle or a young stag. Look! There he stands behind our wall, gazing through the windows, peering through the lattice."

Revelation 3:20 – "Here I am! I stand at the door and knock. If anyone hears my voice and opens the door, I will come in and eat with that person, and they with me."

Stones of Remembrance

There is a reason I recorded the dates I wrote each poem. When the Israelites had an encounter with God, they left stones of remembrance behind to remind them of these different events. Later when they would come upon these stones they would recount why they were there and tell it to their children, (Joshua 4:1-9).

A date at the end of each poem is a stone of remembrance to me, a time when I sat down to be in God's presence and listen for that still small voice in my thoughts. I never want to forget that. For some poems I even remember where I was and can still picture in my mind sitting there and writing them down.

What are your stones of remembrance?

Be Blessed

I sit down and read my poems often. They draw me closer to the Lord. My hope and prayer is that others will feel the Lord speaking to them as they read them. From the time I started writing these poems, I have always felt their message was not only for me, but also for the church, the bride of Christ. Be blessed and know the Lord loves you even more that you can hope or imagine.

Psalm 40:3 – "He put a new song in my mouth, a hymn of praise to our God. Many will see and fear the LORD and put their trust in him."

Chapter 1
Drawing Closer

Refresh Me with Apples

"Refresh me with apples, for I am faint with love"
Is what I whispered one day to the One seated above
A smile crossed His face and He sent a reply
On the wings of an angel did the love letter fly

It spoke of His love, it spoke of His grace
The fruit He sent was sweet to my taste
"I will give you the desires of your heart
As you delight yourself in Me and from sin depart"

"Commit your path to Me and do not stray
For I am your life, the truth and the way
Small is the gate and narrow the road
That leads to life and the heavenly abode"

"Come sit under My shade, get relief from the sun
Partake of the banquet My victory has won
Through the valley of death the path may lead
But I will restore your soul and supply every need"

"Come to the waters that never shall run dry
These streams will flow to those who draw nigh
If anyone is thirsty, let him come drink of Me
And receive life abundant that lasts eternally"

June 18, 2016

Song of Solomon 2:3-5 – "Like an apple tree among the trees of the forest is my beloved among the young men. I delight to sit in his shade, and his fruit is sweet to my taste. ⁴ Let him lead me to the banquet hall, and let his banner over me be love. ⁵ Strengthen me with raisins; refresh me with apples, for I am faint with love."

Psalm 37:3-4
John 14:5-6
Matthew 7:13-14
Psalm 23
John 7:37-39

Speak Lord

Lord, open up my ears to hear
As I invite You to draw near
Still my thoughts that aren't from You
To hear Your words fall as morning dew

I peacefully wait to hear Your voice
To pray and listen requires a choice
For the things of this world are loud and speak
But the thoughts of the Spirit are quiet and meek

Speak, Lord, for the hour is late
The night grows long as I patiently wait
To hear Your voice play a tune on my heart
For the melody to speak and its message impart

May 28, 2016

Psalm 42:1-2 – "As the deer pants for streams of water, so my soul pants for you, my God. ² My soul thirsts for God, for the living God. When can I go and meet with God?"

Hebrews 10:19-22
Isaiah 50:4-5
Psalm 5
Psalm 42

I woke in the middle of the night and couldn't sleep. After wasting an hour on meaningless thoughts, I rose to spend time listening and praying. This poem came to me then. Just as dew appears in the early morning hours, but you can't see it coming, so the Lord's voice appeared and gently landed on my waiting heart.

Prayer: Remind me, Lord, when I can't sleep, to turn to You to hear Your voice and also share my thoughts with You. In this quiet time, away from the busyness of the day, I know You are waiting to visit with me.

I Will Draw Near

Twinkling like diamonds in the starry heights
A swirling cosmos with endless lights
Like eternity stretching without a clear end
Overseeing it all, My Redeemer and Friend

Directing, protecting from His throne in the sky
The heavens can't contain His presence on high
He dwells in eternity, the beginning and end
But does not think it stooping to call me His friend

"Come near Me, draw near Me, abide and stay
While the shadows are lengthening and night turns to day
When the seasons do change, stay close to My side
Safety is there when in Me you abide"

How can I refuse this amazing request?
How can I give anything except my very best?
I will devote myself to my Creator and Friend
And stay close to Him enjoying days without end

I will draw near and never let go
I will draw near content to follow
Enjoying life in the Spirit till my final breath
Till the cord is cut loose and I am free from death

July 29, 2014

"I will bring him near and he will come close to me - for who is he who will devote himself to be close to me?' declares the Lord. "'So you will be my people, and I will be your God.'" Jeremiah 30:21, 22 NIV

2 Chronicles 2:5,6
Psalm 8
Psalm 19
Psalm 91
Ecclesiastes 12:6, 7

While reading Jeremiah 30:21 in my morning devotional, this question from the Lord seemed to leap out and burn itself on my heart, *"for who is he who will devote himself to be close to Me?' declares the Lord"*. Immediately, my response was, "I will, Lord. What a privilege that would be". I even wrote in the margin of my bible, "I will!" beside the verse. As I meditated on that verse, I thought how humbling that must have been of God to ask that question. Then in my mind's eye, I pictured Him on His throne overseeing the cosmos and really needing nothing. Myriads of angels attended to His every need.

Then I asked the Lord, "What is on Your heart, what is it You want me to know"? The verses of this poem started to appear in my head. I couldn't write them down fast enough.

What an awesome privilege that the maker of the universe would ask that question to me! If you are reading this, He is asking that same question to you, *"for who is he who will devote himself to be close to Me?' declares the Lord"*. What is your response?

Prayer: How wonderful that You invite us to be close to You, Lord, and devote ourselves to You. Help us to draw near to where You are in the

Spirit. Thank You for the invitation, it is priceless. We cannot even begin to fathom Your greatness and power. One day we will be where You are and see the wonders of the universe. But, it will be Your presence that will be the greatest marvel of all.

Be Still

Too much activity - going round and round
I need to find quiet to hear God's beckoning sound
It is a voice that calls to me sweet and low
Revealing many things that He wants me to know

Be still my soul and wait for His voice
I want to hear words that cause my heart to rejoice
The joy of the Lord is truly my strength
This joy can be found anywhere across the earth's length

"Come up with Me to high places above
It is in My presence that you'll find true love
A love that is holy, a love that is pure
Will surely be your portion and help you endure"

Be still my soul for the Lord does wait
For me to appear and open the gate
He longs to come in and share my life
I am His betrothed and one day will be His wife

He calls to me from outside my front door
"Come and open My beloved", His voice does implore
"For I long to come in and spend time with you
Till night's shadow passes into morning's dew"

"There you will discover My true heart's desire
As you soak in My presence and the Spirit's bright fire
My glory will shine on your face, in your heart
As we travel the world and this glory impart"

January 14, 2017

Matthew 6:6
Ephesians 2:4-10
Revelation 3:20
Acts 1:4-8
Isaiah 60:1-3

Peace, Peace

Peace, peace was dropped in my soul
A quieted heart instead of turmoil
The news should have startled maybe even upset
But a deep seated peace would not let me fret

In my time of prayer I felt Jesus draw near
"Just rest in faith until the way becomes clear"
He pointed to the future with a smile on His face
"I know the way and will set things in place"

"What do I do now"? I heard me proclaim
"Just draw close to Me", was the answer that came
"For in confidence and rest your faith comes alive
Allowing your spirit to flourish and thrive"

"You are being changed from glory to glory
Eternity will thrill as each tells their story
Of hearts proved true through struggle and pain
For our present sufferings will produce eternal gain"

January 26, 2017

John 14:25-27
Hebrews 11:1
Hebrews 10:35
2 Corinthians 3:17-18
Romans 8:18

Choose This Day

Keep me close to Your heart Oh Lord
That is the prayer from my soul outpoured
It is so easy to drift away
My flesh and my will do so readily stray

Great Shepherd of the flock, You protect
And go after the lost to save and collect
You dry their tears and heal each one
Leading them home when the day is done

The grass is not greener on the other side
Close to the Shepard the flock is content to abide
By the still waters they can hear His voice
The invitation to join this flock is your choice

Jesus is the way, the truth and the life
Outside of the gate is a world filled with strife
The time has come to choose and decide
The place through eternity where forever you'll abide

April 12, 2017

John 10:1-18
John 14:1-6

Joshua 24:14-15 – "Now fear the LORD and serve him with all faithfulness. Throw away the gods your ancestors worshiped beyond the Euphrates River and in Egypt, and serve the LORD. [15] But if serving the LORD seems undesirable to you, then choose for yourselves this day whom you will serve, whether the gods your ancestors served beyond the Euphrates, or the gods of the Amorites, in whose land you are living. But as for me and my household, we will serve the LORD."

Compass Points

As the compass points out true north
Depend on My love as your one true source
Don't be like Israel whose heart went astray
Even though following the cloud that led them by day

Again and again they put God to the test
Vexing the Holy One as they wandered east and west
I long to gather you under My wing
Listening to praises arise as you sing

As warm air comes and the south wind blows
So My Spirit leads and gently flows
Over those whose hearts are pure and meek
Over those who truth and mercy seek

One day I'll return watch the sky in the east
Gathering My bride to the wedding feast
We will dance on streets that are pure gold
Enjoying days without end as eternity unfolds

September 2, 2014

Psalm 78

As I read and meditated on Psalm 78 this poem came to me. I prayed my heart would not be like Israel who went astray. God is so worthy of our love and praises. How He longs for us to turn to Him fully. Our Savior provides everything we need. Look to Him as our one true source, not our disappointment as Israel did.

Prayer: Let my heart be like a compass, Lord, always pointing to You. May I have integrity of heart like David who was fully committed to You. With Your Spirit as my guide, let me not stray off of the high road of holiness.

Matters of the Heart

Rain does fall upon the evil and the just
Let me learn from You and in Your ways trust
Fill me with Your love to cast out my fear
So I can bring help to the lost and those who despair

I want to go deeper in Your Word and get lost in Your love
As I fix my heart on the city that is located above
Show me the way on life's narrow road
As I take up Your cross and share others load

I know of Your deeds, now show me Your way
From your commandments I will not stray
The heart is deceitful above all things
Who can understand the trouble it brings?

My prayer to You in matters of the heart
Is to love through me and from Your ways not depart
They are bound tight together in Your eternal plan
Which existed in eternity even before time began

August 27, 2016

Matthew 5:43-48
1 John 4:16-21
Galatians 6:1-10
Exodus 33:12-14
Psalm 103:7
Jeremiah 17:9
John 14:15-21

Hidden Mysteries of God

So many mysteries hidden in God's word
Eye has not seen nor has the ear heard
Too many to be counted in the span of earth's time
Only eternity will reveal all the secrets sublime

You will find Me when you seek with all of your heart
The fear of the Lord is the place you must start
Ask for My wisdom and learn to obey
Search for My presence in both night and day

I stand afar off from the proud and the vain
Humble yourself and count loss as gain
I am close to the broken, the lame and the blind
Be My eyes and My ears and hands that are kind

I long to hear of your love for Me
Share your thoughts and your lives with Me I plea
Together we will discover hidden mysteries so deep
Ancient treasures long buried is what you will reap

July 23, 2016

1 Corinthians 2:7 – "No, we declare God's wisdom, a mystery that has been hidden and that God destined for our glory before time began."

Proverbs 25:2 – "It is the glory of God to conceal a matter; to search out a matter is the glory of kings."

1 Corinthians 2:6-16
John 21:25
Proverbs 2
Philippians 3:4-11
Psalm 34:18
Isaiah 33:5-6
Matthew 13:44-46
Colossians 2:2-3

Pilgrim's Feet

Doors to Heavenly portals are opened wide
In the city of Jerusalem where the King does abide
Pilgrims ascend with joy in their heart
Open to what the Holy Spirit will impart

From far and wide they come to adore
To seek God's presence and to implore
Prayers and petitions are in their hand
With faith they come to the Holy Land

Heavenly choirs accompany this crowd
While celestial instruments are playing loud
For if they were quiet stones would cry out
The hills would bow down and the valleys would shout

Songs and praise are on their lips
Bags are in hand and babies are on hips
Prayers and petitions are in their hand
With faith they come to the Holy Land

The King does watch from His throne on high
As they gather below and seek to draw nigh
Portals are opened and the Spirit comes down
To those who are gathered in Jerusalem's town

Hope and love they carry inside
To seek His face and in His presence abide
Prayers and petitions are in their hand
With faith they come to the Holy Land

November 15, 2016

Psalm 48
Hebrews 11
Genesis 28:10-22

Waking up in the middle of the night on the first day I was in Jerusalem, this poem came to me. You do not have to go to the Holy Land or Jerusalem though to have pilgrim's feet. Our journey through life is a pilgrimage if our destination is to know the one true God as revealed in the Bible. Hebrews 11:8-16 makes that clear. Since the King is omnipresent, (everywhere at the same time), we can seek His face wherever we are and create portals where the heavens are opened and answers to our prayers cause action in the spirit realm.

When Jacob saw the stairway coming down from heaven in Bethel, (Genesis 28:10-22), his eyes were opened to see in the spirit realm and he saw what was taking place behind the scenes. This activity goes on all the time. We just can't always see it because we are called to walk by faith. There is a special blessing for those who have not seen and yet have believed, (John 20:29).

Prayer: Lord, in this pilgrimage called life, open my eyes and help me to see that we can cause heaven to open by our prayers and praise when we choose to draw closer to You. Faith, hope and love are the keys to these open doors from heaven.

An Angel Waits in Iona

An angel waits in Iona for me
He holds out his hand and bids me, "come see"
Multitudes have traveled this way before
To seek out God's presence and His grace implore

There is only one road only one way
To reach this portal you must not stray
The angels watch over to help you along
The way is paved with praises and song

Ancient hills watch over this most holy throng
Those dedicated - to whom God belong
Mull in your heart - the Lord bids you come
Until you are invited to meet Him when day's work is done

May 2, 2017

Matthew 7:13-14
Hebrews 1:14
2 Peter 1:13-15
2 Kings 2:1-18

In 2017 I went on a trip to Ireland and Scotland. When in Scotland we traveled to an island called Mull. We got off the ferry and stayed at this large hotel nearby. The next morning we traveled across the island to another small island called Iona. Someone told me that there was only one road in Mull that leads to Iona. And this road is only one way. If another car came from the other direction you had to pull off on the side of the roads in places.

Before we got to Iona the leader, Kathy, told us that there were many angel visitations and miracles on this island for many centuries. She said the veil between heaven and earth is very thin in this area. I pictured in my mind or had an impression of an angel waiting for me in Iona. I did not see it with my eyes. I pictured this angel holding out his hand and pointing to something to show me. Immediately the words to this poem started to come to me. I finished it before we got to the island.

The Saint, Columba, established a monastery on this island of Iona. He was said to have done many miracles and had many angelic visitations. A great revival broke out in his lifetime and many people came to the Lord. One of the things that were written about these saints living back then was that when their time of death approached sometimes the Lord would reveal their day of departing to them. They called this an invitation from the Lord. It was an invitation to return to Him. That is what they called their homecoming, an invitation from the Lord.

Debbie Furey

The Magi's Gifts

Gold, it tells a kingly story
Of how You left Your home in glory
And came to earth to suffer shame
To bear our sins and take the blame

Myrrh, it breathes a sweet perfume
It covers over death and gloom
Reminding us You took our place
Imparting fragrance, love and grace

In Frankincense, a cloud appears
Ascending upwards like our prayers
Touching heaven's throne with power
Releasing angels and God's fire

All of these tell a story
Of the Fathers love and glory
Drawing us to Him in love
Respond to Him who reigns above

Let us fall now on our knees
Present to Him our prayers and pleas
Gaze on Him who reigns above
Deserving of our lives, our love

As in life, it was in death
These gifts we offer with our breath
Symbolic now we give to Thee
Accept them from our hands we plea

Friday, March 20, 2014

Mathew 2
John 19:39
Exodus 30:34-38
Judges 13:19,20
Song of Solomon 3:6

After writing the poem down, I asked the Lord, what do You mean, "As in life, it was in death"? The answer I got, "Just as the Magi gave Me gifts at the beginning of My life, so I received the same gifts at My death. The gold represented My burial in a rich man's tomb. The myrrh was put in My burial cloth to cover the smell of death. And frankincense and oil was added to the "Bread of Life" as My body was being prepared as an offering to the Father on high.

I was also puzzled why in March, I received a poem that seemed to be about Christmas. The answer was, "as in life, it was in death". The Lenten season I am in now is a preparation of the foretelling of the death of Jesus. Symbolically, now, we can give these same gifts to Him.

For gold, we can give a special offering to a missionary or our church. The giving of frankincense represents our prayers ascending to God as a sweet smelling offering. And for myrrh we can go without, give up something, or fast. It is a picture of dying to self.

Prayer: Oh God, so many times I have received a scripture or a word from You that seemed "out of season". I tossed it aside like I must have heard wrong, without meditating on it or understanding what You were trying to tell me. Forgive me for not always being in tune with You, and Your Spirit. Help me to die to self, so I might awaken my spirit more to hear Your still small voice.

The Bridegroom's Song

My child of morning, pure delight
Thy prayers are precious in My sight
Come and join Me in the dance
Come and join Me for romance

My love is sure, My love is pure
My love is meant to last, endure
Sweet breath of dew that does appear
Then is no more, but do not fear

Your heart is beating next to Mine
Your heart I will like gold refine
Till all that's left is tried and true
Till all of Me is seen in you

Take My hand, My heart is thine
Tis full of love and truth divine
Come and join Me in the dance
Come and join Me for romance

August 7, 2010

Song of Solomon 2
Malachi 3:2-4
James 4:13-15

As I started to write this poem, I saw in my spirit, the Bridegroom, with His hand outstretched, inviting us (as the bride of Christ) to dance with Him. I couldn't see Him clearly, but I knew He was the Lord. I knew this poem was not addressed to me personally, as much as it was an invitation to His church, the bride.

The invitation to dance and romance speaks of intimacy. It also means to be in step with Him and let Him lead. This is His song to you.

Prayer: I give You my hand, my heart, my life. Lead me in the way You would have me to go. I will follow.

Chapter 2
A Repentant Heart

A Repentant Heart

You promise, "every morning My mercies are new"
Your faithfulness falls on me as morning dew
As a new day begins afresh with life
My heart is washed clean from yesterday's strife

Create a perfect heart in me O Lord
As I regularly bathe in the truth of Your Word
A repentant heart is the place to start
So heaven can open and Your truth impart

There is no place I would rather be
Than sitting at Your feet listening devotedly
My heart acknowledges God's way is right
A repentant heart can restore my sight

O God, Your judgments are true and just
On Your mercy I can depend and trust
The path I take leads to heaven's door
This will open to joy and life evermore

October 28, 2016

Lamentations 3:21-26
Psalm 51
Revelation 16:7

Luke 7:29-30 – "All the people, even the tax collectors, when they heard Jesus' words, acknowledged that God's way was right, because they had been baptized by John. [30] But the Pharisees and the experts in the law rejected God's purpose for themselves, because they had not been baptized by John."

As I was reading Luke 7:29-30 this morning it revealed to me an amazing thing. A repentant heart is what opens people's eyes to see that God's way is right. Without that we will reject God's purpose for our lives.

John's baptism was for repentance. He had to precede Jesus because repentance was what opened the people's eyes to the truth Jesus was proclaiming. The ones who rejected Jesus' message were the Pharisees and they are the ones who had not been baptized by John, showing they did not have repentant hearts. They trusted in their own right standing with God and denied they have any sin to repent of.

A repentant heart opens our eyes to truth.

Prayer: Oh Lord, I repent for all the times I was self-righteous and walking in darkness. Open my eyes to see the sin in my life so I can judge myself and turn from my wicked ways. I acknowledge God's ways are right and just. Show me the path and purpose You have for my life. Thank You for dying on the cross for me and taking my place to fulfill the wrath of a holy God.

Return, Return

My heart is grieved for My sons who are fallen
For they have rejected Me and refused My calling
They would have ridden on the high places of the earth
Had the privilege of suffering for My purposes to birth

For some of My called ones have chosen to play
When they need to be working in the harvest for that "Day"
I am coming soon and My reward is with Me
For some the door will open and their eyes will see

A storm is approaching and there is not much time
The clock hand approaches twelve and is about to chime
For the kings of the earth do plot in vain
But One enthroned above holds them in disdain

The earth is Mine and I am coming to claim
Those who are waiting, whose hearts are aflame
So I will pour out My mercy, grace and love
To those who are working for treasure above

Return, return – those who have fallen
Please open your heart and hear Me calling
It is not too late to return to the field
To pick up My yoke and to My ways yield

September 8, 2016

Revelation 22:12
Hebrews 10:19-39
Philippians 1:29
Philippians 3:7-11
1 Peter 4:12-19
John 4:34-38
Matthew 25:10-13
Psalm 2
Matthew 11:28-30

The Father's Tears

Who collects the Father's tears?
Shed throughout eternity's years
They would have formed a river wide
For from His eyes can nothing hide

The Father's heart is deep and vast
It holds eternity in its grasp
Within its depths was each created
And in His book was each life dated

His Father's heart calls out "Return"
For of His ways must each one learn
Left on our own we all do stray
From off the path marked "narrow way"

He knows the way we take and weeps
For what we sow in life we reap
He longs to gather us under His wings
Where each one's safe and joyfully sings

Each must choose – we have a free will
His children have a destiny to fulfill
Praise Him who all our sorrow bears
But who collects the Father's tears?

September 23, 2016

"You number my wanderings; put my tears into Your bottle; are they not in Your book?" Psalm 56:8 NKJV

2 Chronicles 16:9
Revelation 20:11-14
Matthew 7:13-14
Luke 13:34

   A practice in olden times was for mourners to catch their tears in bottles or water skins and put them at the tombs of their loved ones. The Psalmist is referring to this practice and even indicates they are written down in heaven's books recorded for all time.

Yesterday I found an old journal of mine and read a passage I had long forgotten about. Because of a deep hurt in my heart I was crying in the shower. The release of those tears felt strangely good as I quietly sobbed and let my tears mingle with the shower of cleansing water.

It was then that I heard a quiet voice in my thoughts that wasn't my own saying, "How do you expect Me to separate all those tears from the water coming down?"

I knew instantly what He meant and it made me smile because I knew that He was there, close beside me, and that He cared.

As my body slowly stopped shaking from my sobbing, I found myself with a smile on my face that wouldn't let go. You see, I know God can do anything, but the mental image of Him or His angels separating those tears from the water as they were falling and bottling them was so amusing I had to laugh.

How deep is the Lord's love!

I sensed that so fully from His small teasing statement as He urged me from a sense of despair, to a deeper level of faith in Him and in His love for me.

Then, as I was in prayer this morning pondering over yesterday's old journal entry, I suddenly wondered, "Who collects the Father's tears?" That is when this poem came to me.

Prayer: Lord, we cannot comprehend Your love for us, yet You try to show it to us in so many ways. Help us to show our love to You in our thoughts and everyday life. We want to bring a smile to Your face.

Choose Life

Sin does something to your heart
A little less holy, a little less smart
A cold long finger snuffs out a flame
Replacing it with guilt and shame
Nothing was gained, something was lost
Count the cost…..Count the cost

Eternity will reveal the theft
Before God's throne there's nothing left
When our treasures we before Him bring
Praises to the most High King
Worthy, worthy to the Lamb on high
Sin dulls God's voice here below the skies

Don't you chance it, live and learn!
Mercy has come that you did not earn
Pouring from God's heart comes clean and strong
Grace's healing balm to reverse any wrong
Therefore, return soon to the path of life
Angels wait to help you enter the light.

Thursday October 18, 2012

1 Corinthians 3:10-17
1 Peter 1:13-25
1 Peter 2:1-12
1 Peter 4
1 John 1:5-7

This poem is about continuing in sin. There is a choice here. Don't miss it. Eternity will reveal the cost.

Prayer: Lead me by Your Spirit, Lord. Open my eyes to the sin in my heart. Help me to judge myself of my sins. We are a chosen people, a royal priesthood, and we need to start walking on the path of life with repentance and humility as befits the people of God. Angels are watching.

1 Peter 1:10-12 – "Concerning this salvation, the prophets, who spoke of the grace that was to come to you, searched intently and with the greatest care, [11] trying to find out the time and circumstances to which the Spirit of Christ in them was pointing when he predicted the sufferings of the Messiah and the glories that would follow. [12] It was revealed to them that they were not serving themselves but you, when they spoke of the things that have now been told you by those who have preached the gospel to you by the Holy Spirit sent from heaven. Even angels long to look into these things.

Our Wicked Hearts

The heart is quite wicked its depth we can't know
Take heed for out it the issues of life flow
Like a volcano whose lava bursts forth from its top
The secrets of our hearts will from our mouths drop

A well cannot produce water both bitter and sweet
One day our words will be weighed at God's judgment seat
Our thoughts will be revealed to all gathered there
God's Word will be proved true so we need to beware

Therefore, I invite the Holy Spirit to start
Convict me of sin and cleanse my dirty heart
Create in me a clean heart Oh Lord
Where Your Word can dwell richly and then be outpoured

I want life giving waters to flow out of me
To quench those who are thirsty and to set people free
It starts by acknowledging the sin in my heart
Choosing God's way and from sin depart

March 14, 2017

Jeremiah 17:9-10 (NKJV) – "The heart *is* deceitful above all *things,* and desperately wicked; who can know it? [10] I, the LORD, search the heart; I test the mind, even to give every man according to his ways, according to the fruit of his doings."

Proverbs 4:23
James 3:9-12
Matthew 12:33-37
1 Corinthians 4:5
Psalm 51

Set Me Free

Lord, take away my bent to sin
Help me run the race to win
Free me from what holds me back
Supply the gifts I sorely lack

My heart, it yearns to run to You
Refresh my soul like morning dew
For swirling mists around me rise
Trapping fears, guilt, shame and lies

Debbie Furey

Let me see You face to face
Impart Your mercy, love and grace
It is in Your presence I am set free
To be who You created me to be

Come shine Your light within my soul
Expose the sin which takes a toll
Come live within my spirit deep
Whether wide awake or fast asleep

Set me free to live with You
Within my mind, transform, renew
I offer You myself, my life
Accept me as a living sacrifice

July 14, 2016

Acts 20:24
1 Corinthians 9:24-27
Galatians 5:7-26
Hebrews 12:1-4
Romans 12:1-2

To Him Who Overcomes

Lord, I run to You in my defeat
And plead for grace at Your mercy seat
Repeated failures can turn my heart to stone
If not for Your forgiveness, at the mercy throne

The angels carry God's message of forgiveness and love
To those on their knees in repentance thereof
The Lord is looking for those with a perfect heart
So, humility and honesty is the place to start

We can overcome by the blood of the Lamb
For our heavenly Advocate is the great "I AM"
He intercedes for us from His throne on high
So don't you give up and believe the lie

To him who overcomes will I give a white stone
For to live in your sin I will never condone
Repent, therefore, for I am coming back soon
With My double-edged sword emitting a sorrowful tune

To him who overcomes will I give some hidden manna
Your mournful words will be changed to "hosanna"
A new name will be given that I alone know
My hand to My pure bride I will joyfully bestow

August 30, 2016

Psalm 51
Revelation 12:11
Revelation 2:12-17
Ephesians 5:25-27

Humble Yourselves

There is a great cost to following the Lord
Some have been martyred through flames or the sword
Persecution can come through wagging tongues and narrowed eyes
But it all serves to humble those, who to self, want to die

Humble yourselves under My mighty hand
That I may help you to possess your promised land
For I am far from the proud and will not hear their cry
Until they humble themselves and to the world die

Take up My cross for I am lowly and meek
Those who are yielded and love Me I seek
For if you gain the whole world what good would it be?
If you would forfeit your soul and be forever without Me?

March 9, 2017

Hebrews 11
1 Peter 5:6
Matthew 10:38-39
Matthew 16:24-26
Matthew 22:1-14
2 Chronicles 7:14

David and Bathsheba's Restoration

A melody arose from David's lips
And flowed from his harp through his fingertips
A song of mercy, a song of love
Came to him from God above

It spoke of cleansing, hope and grace
From his sins, God would hide His face
Sins recorded in the Book of Life
Were blotted out when repentance sufficed

"A perfect heart, create in me"
The grateful king to God did plea
"Restore to me Your Spirit and joy
That I had with You since I was a boy"

"Then I will teach transgressors Your ways
Repaying Your mercy till my final days
My tongue will sing of Your righteousness and truth
So that sinners will return, both the old and youth"

A broken spirit and a contrite heart
You will not despise or Your grace depart
Love so amazing, forgiving and pure
Will be celebrated forever and endure

What You did for David, You will do for me
So I can be with You throughout eternity
Rejoicing in Your forgiveness and grace
As a queen by Your side in that hallowed place

December 11, 2014

Psalm 51

Psalm 51 is about King David repenting for the sins of adultery with Bathsheba and the murder of her husband. While reading the kings heartbroken and contrite words this morning, the thought came to me of how the royal lineage was passed down through Solomon, the son of David and Bathsheba. He had many other wives and sons whom the crown could have gone to. Why, I wondered, did God choose Solomon, son of Bathsheba, a symbol of David's greatest personal failing"?

A still small voice answered me, "so that future generations would know I answered David's prayer to blot out his sin and iniquity and remember it no more. When I look at David, I do not remember his failings, but his perfect heart for Me".

Yes, David did have to suffer the consequences of his sin during his lifetime, the effects which were very severe. But, during these events, a clear picture of the love, mercy and forgiveness of God emerges toward David and Bathsheba, so much so that God chooses their offspring to be in the lineage of Jesus, the light of the world, who would save the people from their sin.

Prayer: Lord, I am humbled by Your deep love and forgiveness toward us. It staggers the mind and heart. This forgiveness You displayed toward David is available to us if we repent and turn from our sins also. Please help us to love and forgive others in the same way, so that others can see You in us.

Chapter 3
Faith, Hope and Love

Faith, Hope and Love

As a moth is drawn to fire's domain
My heart returns to You again and again
The fire of Your presence fills my soul with delight
As faith is transformed from hope into sight

For hope that is seen is no hope at all
But to count hope as seen releases faith great and small
In this hope we are saved and changed day by day
As Your love is poured into vessels made of clay

Love is not seen until it is given away
This makes room for more of God's love to display
Now I will show you the most excellent way
Love fulfills the law so be careful to obey

Return to the path of life and do not stray
So the world can see God's glory in our lives everyday
There is much strife that comes; it can cause us to fall
Remember to love, it is the greatest of all

Fire of God's presence, come fill my soul with delight
As my faith is transformed from hope into sight
Draw me closer to You again and again
Till I am seated with You forever to reign.

May 7, 2016

1 Corinthians 13:13 – "And now these three remain: faith, hope and love. But the greatest of these is love."

Song of Solomon 2:3-5
Hebrews 11:1-3
Romans 8:24-25
1 Corinthians 13
Ephesians 2:1-10

Sensing Your Presence

My eyes can't see You, but I sense You are there
For it is by faith that I know You are everywhere
Your perfumed presence my nose can't detect
So I'll search for You daily and will not neglect

I have tasted Your goodness and do not lack
It is Your grace and mercy that keep me coming back
A still small voice gently whispers to me
As I quiet myself and wait patiently

The Lord has touched my heart, I am not the same
Knowing He died for my sins and took the blame
With His arms opened wide He invites me "come near"
"Abide under My wings and cast off your fear"

"For I will be with you always until the end
Then you will enter eternity as My bride and My friend
Now I am behind the lattice, waiting at the door
It will soon be opened, a new life to explore"

May 13, 2015

Hebrews 11:1-3
Song of Solomon 1:3,13,14
Psalm 45:8
Psalm 34:8-10
Psalm 46:10
Psalm 91:1-6
Matthew 28:20
Song of Solomon 2:9-10
Matthew 25:6-10

While reading the first chapter of Song of Solomon this morning, I wondered what the Lord might smell like. This passage as well as Psalm 45:8 describe the intoxicating fragrance of the Bridegroom. One day we will find out what was so captivating a scent. One day we will see Him, hear His voice and feel His touch. For now, we can only imagine. The Lord promised a special blessing for those who don't see Him, but believe. Through our eyes of faith we can see the results of His love for us in changed lives, His provision for us, and His care of us. Jesus is coming soon.

Prayer: Lord, let us sense Your presence around us. As we feed on Your word, fill us with Your Holy Spirit. Help us to hear Your still, small voice and see You in other people. Help us to touch their lives with Your love. Let them smell Your fragrance of love lingering on us.

Revelation 22:17, 20
"The Spirit and the bride say, "Come!" And let the one who hears say, "Come!" Let the one who is thirsty come; and let the one who wishes take the free gift of the water of life."
"He who testifies to these things says, "Yes, I am coming soon."
Amen. Come, Lord Jesus.

Contagious Faith to Battle Giants

Do not fear though there are giants in the land
I, the Lord, am your shield, behind Me stand
Look down in the brook and see the five stones
Reach down in faith, though it seems you're alone

Remember your victory over the lion and bear
I was with you then so you need not despair
I've trained your fingers for battle and your hands for war
To conquer the giants you must walk through the door

The door is called faith you know not where it leads
Though the way seems dark I will supply every need
The path will teach you, I am the way, truth and life
Keep your eyes on Me through the battles and strife

This path of life is a narrow way
Dangerous ditches on each side lay
Snares and traps are there to lure the weak
Humility and love are the protection of the meek

Your faith will be contagious to those on that road
I have sent them that way to lighten your load
My mighty army is gathering to make a stand
To take back the land from the enemies hand

When Israel saw that Goliath was dead
Their faith came alive replacing the dread
They took up their arms and pursued with a shout
Hope sprung anew replacing their doubt

Faith is contagious so stay close to Me
It comes from hearing My words, so listen closely
Ask for My wisdom and learn to obey
Come into My presence, abide and stay

Your thoughts are not My thoughts says the Lord
I am your commander, pick up your sword
March toward the giants My praises declare
Take back the land, the victory we'll share

September 5, 2014

1 Samuel 17
Psalm 3
Romans 10:17

David picked up five stones in the brook on the way to meet the giant. He knew Goliath had four other brothers and wanted to be prepared. As it turned out, the other giants were killed later by David's men. I think they figured if David could do it they could also. If you read between the lines, David's mighty men were very competitive. They saw his relationship with God and wanted it also. God was with them as with David. For you see, faith is contagious.

Before David killed the giant, he had a test with the lion and bear. A person would not usually survive either encounter. Through those victories David relied on the Lord and trusted Him to protect him. It was a training of sorts to prepare him for the battles ahead and to teach him to fight. Though they were formidable, David prevailed.

Don't be afraid of what comes against you. Use your faith to overcome. It will protect you like a shield. Pick up your sword, which is the word of God and march toward the giants in your land. Your faith will be contagious to those around you. Victory is sure.

Prayer: You said to ask for wisdom, Lord, so I am asking. On my own, I can't win any battle. I need Your presence. When You show up, humility and love are there in abundance. I want what You have. Please protect me from foes who are much stronger than I am. In faith, I am depending on You.

Hope Rises Up

There is a song in my heart when I think of You
When I recall all You did and all You will do
Hope rises up like a balloon released to flight
From that vantage point faith turns into sight

You raised me up with Christ and seated me on high
By grace I am saved and invited to draw nigh
In coming ages we will see the riches of His grace
Brought into His kingdom where the redeemed will see His face

No mourning will be there, no death, pain or tears
Time will not be counted in minutes, hours or years
Eternal joy will be released like water from a dam
When we behold the sacred face of the great "I AM"

March 17, 2017

Hebrews 11:1-2
Ephesians 2:4-10
Exodus 33:11
Psalm 24:3-10
Revelation 21

Follow the Way of Love

A song of victory, a song of love
Came down to me from God above
Its melody soft with golden glory
Played a tune, a wistful story

Look through eyes of love to see
That people are not what they seem to be
How easy to judge their thoughts and ways
Without knowing what their yearning heart says

Love is patient, love is kind
Like treasure in a field it is hard to find
When one truly has it, love must be given away
For others to see love, it must be displayed

Where do we find this treasure so rare?
What do we possess that can even compare?
You will find Me when you search with all of your heart
For it is in My presence, My love I impart

Come to the well that will never run dry
This living water is for those who draw nigh
As you are refreshed draw some water for others
For the whole human race are really our brothers

I died for them all so My love they could share
One way they can know this is they see that you care
To follow the way of love – is to follow Me
The path that I take leads to life abundantly

Stay close to Me and walk by My side
You will have love for others when in Me you abide
Experience the flow of My mercy and grace
As your heart turns to Me and we speak face to face

May 24, 2016

1 Corinthians 13   Matthew 13:44
Matthew 16:24-27   John 4:4-15
John 3:16-21   John 15:1-17
Exodus 33:11

Winter's Beauty Sings

The snow falls gently on my soul
Masking winters harsh death toll
The soft white puffs brighten grays gloom
Erasing the dreary with heaven's broom

How can such weight fall without a thud?
And muffle loud sounds and cover mud?
Snow robes the trees with different splendor
Than summer's coat of leaves so tender

"Don't despair", its message brings
Even winter's beauty sings
The praise and wonder of God's creation
Speaks to us even through tribulation

December 30, 2016

2 Corinthians 4:16-18 – "Therefore we do not lose heart. Though outwardly we are wasting away, yet inwardly we are being renewed day by day. [17] For our light and momentary troubles are achieving for us an eternal glory that far outweighs them all. [18] So we fix our eyes not on what is seen, but on what is unseen, since what is seen is temporary, but what is unseen is eternal."

Job 38:22-30
Philippians 4:4-9

Looking out the window while sitting and waiting to hear God's voice, the snow had just started falling. Winter is not my favorite time of the year. Certain seasons we go through in life can also be just as barren and cold, but beauty can be found in these trials if we see them through God's eyes. There is purpose in everything we go through – even the winters of our lives, those times when it is cold and dreary, those times when we crave warmth and comfort. One day we will understand and see the whole picture. Until then we rest in faith and hope which has much beauty in God's eyes.

Debbie Furey

Prayer – Lord, help me to see things through Your eyes. Your word promises that all things work together for good to those who love God. So thank You and I praise You for all that I am going through because there is a purpose in everything.

Prayer for the New Year

Bring out the old, ring in the new
One year passing, another year due
Lord, teach us to number our days aright
So that we may be blameless and holy in Your sight

Help us let go of the past with its flaws
Repent of the sins that went against Your laws
Relent, O Lord! How long will it be?
Till we feel Your compassion, grace and mercy

Satisfy us this New Year with Your unfailing love
That we may sing for joy to the Lord above
Refresh us with Your presence in the form of rain
To end the drought of guilt and shame

From everlasting to everlasting You are God
You know the path I will take and the way I have trod
Surround me with Your presence stay close to my side
As I step forward in faith and in the Vine abide

December 31, 2014

Psalm 90
John 15:1-17

    As I sat in prayer this morning, I asked the Lord for a poem for the New Year. I felt led to read Psalm 90. This is the poem that came to me.

Chapter 4
Follow the Spirit

Follow the Spirit on Eagles Wings

Step out of the nest, oh little one
The day is far spent, the battle not won
Spread your wings and learn how to fly
Rise up in faith, give the victory cry

Learn how to soar on the thermals that rise
Follow the Spirit into clear skies
Higher and higher where the enemy can't go
Till you reach the high peaks laden with snow

Come, stay with Me, in high places above
Learn to reign with Me, absorb My love
Take your fill of My mercy, truth, and grace
Follow the Spirit with the wind in your face

Go where He leads, to the battle below
You are not alone, the others will follow
The enemy is crafty and plans they do make
Terror now fills them, for eagles eat snake

Follow the Spirit, oh loved one, take wing
Soar up with wisdom, His praises now sing
For victory is sure, though the battle be long
Your Redeemer is mighty, majestic and strong

May 16, 2014

Psalm 103:1-5
Isaiah 31:5
Isaiah 40:28-31
Job 38:22, 23
Revelation 12:14

Isaiah 40:29-31 – "He gives strength to the weary and increases the power of the weak. youths grow tired and weary, and young men stumble and fall; but those who hope in the Lord will renew their strength. They will soar on wings like eagles; they will run and not grow weary, they will walk and not be faint."

As I sat down to pray and this poem came to me, I had the impression that we are still small eagles, and not as mature as we think we are. We are not even out of the nest yet. Great victories are in store for us as we step out in faith and learn to fly and follow the Spirit.

The day of the great battle is approaching, but we still have much to learn. All we have learned so far has only been preparation for what is to come.

As we are seated with Christ in heavenly places, there are places spiritual opposing forces can't go. The closer we draw to Christ, who is seated above, the less the enemy can harass us. Enemy birds can harass eagles in flight, but, they have to drop off as eagles rise in flight because they can't go up as high.

When we reach the high peaks laden with snow that is the place the Lord shows us the battle strategies and weapons He has stored for the battle below. See Job 38:22, 23, Joshua 10:11, Exodus 9:23-26 and Revelation 16:21. To see this though, requires us to ascend to where Christ is seated above. We need to ascend before we descend to the battle.

As eagles soar, their cry instills fear in the heart of their enemies. The shrill call pierces the heavens and goes before them. Speak out in faith which is our cry of victory. Before the battle, declare in faith God's promises, declare God's praises. The enemy will tremble, for he knows the praises are true.

Prayer: Yes, Lord, we will follow You out of the nest into the wind of the Spirit. As Your breath fills our wings, we pray it will lead us into Your presence, filling us with Your love, truth, mercy and grace. Let praise fill our mouth, for that is the victory cry of faith. Thank You for Your full provision of all our needs.

Angels Assist Us

Angels assist us on the path of life
They are sent to help us through the battles and strife
At times they protect us when we trip on a stone
In times when we suffer and feel all alone

Angels are dispatched from the throne of grace
They shine with the glory of beholding God's face
On wings of mercy and love they do fly
To return to earth's realm to answer your cry

God knows everything and the way we will take
He knows the plans that our enemies do make
They all fit together in His eternal plan
To form us in His likeness in our inner man

Do not be afraid to go where He sends
For angels go with us to help and defend
The way may be hard and filled with trouble and pain
But the reward is great and we have heaven to gain

June 9, 2016

Matthew 18:10 - "See that you do not despise one of these little ones. For, I tell you that their angels in heaven always see the face of my Father in heaven."

Psalm 91:9-16
Hebrews 1:7, 14
Hebrews 13:1-2
Acts 12:6-10

I Will Follow

Lord:
Step out of the boat and come walk with Me
Tread on the waves in the tempest tossed sea
Nothing can harm you with Me by your side
Speak to the storm and cause it to hide

Me:
Where is thy victory, oh death, thy sting?
If in Jesus, my soul is resting
Storm clouds may threaten and even bring fear
But nothing can hurt me when my Savior is near

Lord:
Draw near to Me, rest under My wing
Open your mouth, My praises to sing
For I am Your provider, guardian and stay
Follow Me closely as I lead the way

Me:
Lead on, oh Master, where else can I go?
Your love has captured my heart, so I will follow
Whether up to the mountain, or down to the sea
My place is with You and forever will be

May 24, 2014

Matthew 8:23-27
John 14:12-14
1 Corinthians 15:55
Psalm 139

Psalm 139:6-10 - "Such knowledge is too wonderful for me; It is high, I cannot attain it. Where can I go from Your Spirit? Or where can I flee from Your presence? If I ascend into heaven, You are there; If I make my bed in hell, behold, You are there. If I take the wings of the morning, And dwell in the uttermost parts of the sea, Even there Your hand shall lead me, And Your right hand shall hold me."

Approaching the second anniversary of my husband's death, the Lord comforted me by having His word "Where is thy victory, oh death, thy sting?" appear often the past few days- in songs, in my mind, in the sermon, etc. I was comforted by the fact I would see Harvey again one day, and the sting of death was softened by the victory of the resurrection of Jesus and His triumph over death. Since the funeral, the Lord has proved His faithfulness to me.

I thought back to all the many changes I have made these past two years. I feel like these changes have positioned me to move forward in a completely new direction at this stage of my life. It will take courage and energy, but I am willing. I just pray to hear clearly so I can follow.

I know it will be a way I haven't gone before, which will take faith. I know it will involve traveling, but I don't know where. I know the Lord will be there guiding me, that is all that matters.

How wonderful to sit in the Lord's presence and hear loving and comforting words of love. As we spend time with Him in our daily walk, He doesn't just want to hear from us, He wants us to listen, to hear what is in His heart. It might be direction or just words of love, but it is true communication. Heart to heart talks, comfort, strength, that is what you will also receive; time is not wasted, only believe.

Prayer: You are the Lord of the universe, but yet You bend low to enter and hear my prayers. Even when I cannot feel Your presence, Your Word promises You are there.

Special Reflection:

A little over a year after I wrote this poem, I went on a cruise with my friend, Margie, who gets motion sickness very easily. The first night at the dinner table, people were discussing the news that a hurricane was heading our way and would arrive shortly. As we were walking on the deck watching the seas grow more restless, my friend started feeling sick.

Then a verse entered my mind from one of the poems I had wrote, "Speak to the storm and cause it to hide". I couldn't remember which poem at the time, but it was repeated in my mind again.

I told Margie so we prayed right there and spoke to the storm and told it to go away in a different direction. A few hours later we prayed that again. The seas calmed down soon after, and the hurricane never did come our way.

Set Sail

To abide under the shadow of Your wing
Is the place I am set free to sing
Of Your marvelous love and holy grace
A place to reach up and touch Your face

This is a day of grace, but also of faith
Set sail, hold fast to run the race
It's not for the strong or the worldly wise*
For they trample My mercy and My grace despise

Set sail, set sail, and let the wind blow
Pull up anchor and do not be afraid to go
For I am beside thee and together we will go
Throughout the whole world for My glory to show

My answer:
You are worthy, You are worthy, O Lord of my heart
I will follow, I will follow – show me where to start
Do not fail to go with me or show me the lead
Keep me as the apple of Your eye I will forever plead

February 13, 2010

*But God chose the foolish things of the world to shame the wise; God chose the weak things of the world to shame the strong. He chose the lowly things of this world and the despised things— and the things that are not— to nullify the things that are, so that no one may boast before him.

1 Corinthians 1:27-29
Psalm 91

A New Path

Behold! A door – it opens wide
Inviting me to come inside
A nail scarred hand beckons me in
A foreboding darkness breathes within

With trembling steps I slowly approach
"Don't be afraid", comes a gentle reproach
"For when one door opens, another must close
You must leave behind the familiar and go"

"Tis' a fearful thing to go a new way
A new era's dawning of a bright new day
Look behind you, a sunset, the old must die
Ahead of you, a sunrise fills the sky"

"The way looks dark now because you cannot see
The path requires faith, My grace and mercy
You must walk in love and the fear of the Lord
My Spirit will lead you, the compass My Word"

"The trail will lead over hill and dale
With many a trial, but you cannot fail
For I will be close, your hope and your friend
And will be with you always, even to the end."

April 5, 2014

John 14

It was almost two years since the passing of my husband, Harvey. One morning as I sat quietly reading my bible, many thoughts were filling my mind, and they didn't seem to match. An open door, the fear of the Lord, letting go of the past were just a few of these fleeting images coming into my thoughts. "What are you trying to tell me," I asked the Lord? As I sat quietly waiting, this poem came to mind.

Prayer: Thank you, Lord, for showing yourself as the Way, the Truth, and the Life. Help me to keep on the path of life, the way of holiness. Keep me in Your Word, so that I may obey You in all things. Reveal Yourself to me through the people I come into contact with, and the events of the day. Help me to feel Your presence.

My Sheep

My sheep hear My voice and follow Me
Green pastures await so abundant and free
They are safe and secure under My watchful eye
Their young can frolic and peacefully lie

Sheep tend to wander and leave the fold
Then lose their way in the dark and cold
The Shepherd follows after to rescue and return
He is guided by their cry and heartfelt yearn

The wolf is watching and comes to steal
He is hungry and searching who will be his next meal
The enemy tries to isolate one from the flock
But mighty is He – our Great Shepherd and Rock

Help me to follow Your way and Your voice
It will matter through eternity, this day's choice
Do not be afraid for our Savior does lead
We must follow closely and to His Word take heed

May 5, 2017

Psalm 23
Psalm 78:52-55
Isaiah 40:10-11
Matthew 6:19-21
Luke 12:32-48
1 Timothy 6:11-21

On a bus trip to Ireland and Scotland in the spring of 2017 I saw many sheep with new born lambs in fenced pastures with no shepherds nearby. It was a delight to see these new lambs resting, frolicking and nursing. Most were white, some black, some mixed in color. My favorite lambs were the white ones with black legs and faces.

In a lot of countries though, because of dense population, the flocks of sheep have to roam around to find enough pasture to eat. They can't just eat anywhere and some are close to towns.

On this trip I met a woman, Elizabeth, from Hoesbach, Germany who was a shepherd in her youth for about two years. There were not fenced meadows for the flocks of sheep so she had to stay with the sheep and carefully watch them all the time. She had to lead them from one pasture to another as the food dwindled. The sheep had to follow her as she led them on roads that went through towns and across bridges. Sheep are very fearful but they learned to trust her because she took them to fresh pastures and protected them. Because she called to them often they got used to her voice and would not follow another.

Sheep have to eat at least eight hours a day because their mouths are so small. Because they have their eyes down to eat they followed each other. If another person walked by at the same pace they could easily follow them because they thought it was their shepherd's legs. So sometimes they got off on the wrong path. But when the shepherd spoke, they always would run after her.

She could tell if they were listening because their ears would move forward. If they were stubborn and refused to listen their ears would turn back and they would not obey her.

One thing Elizabeth noticed was that sheep recognized their lambs by their voice and smell only. They did not seem to be able to recognize their lambs at all by sight, even though the colors were very different. Jesus tells us not to judge by our eyes because we cannot discern correctly. He only listened and did what His Father told Him to do. Also, the Bible tells us that we would know each other by our fruit. Ripe fruit gives off a delightful smell that we can recognize what tree it came from. Matthew 7:15-20.

Elizabeth loved her sheep and ate and slept with them watching over them all the time. They usually socialized with each other and had their eyes down a lot, but every once in a while she caught some of them watching her and wanting to be near her. Her heart just melted with love when that happened. What a beautiful picture she was to me of our loving Shepherd, Jesus.

The Way

There is a way that seems right to a man
So he makes preparations to follow this plan
This path may go smooth or it may be rough
Things might come easy or at times be tough

Each man has a destiny he was born to fulfill
There are no accidents for God has a will
Into each life is a God given breath
Our days are recorded in a book until death

Each goes his way along the path of life
Some days are good, others filled with strife
Then we come to crossroads where each must decide
Whether to seek out the Lord or whether to hide

God's heart searches out the weak and the lost
Do you have any idea what this plan cost?
It was gladly paid on a faraway hill
Our Redeemer was mighty His plan to fulfill

But we must choose His plan and His way
Our eternity depends on our hearts true sway
There is a way that seems right to a man
Will we choose our own path or go with God's plan?

August 4, 2016

John 14:6 – "Jesus answered, "I am the way and the truth and the life. No one comes to the Father except through me."

Proverbs 14:12 (NKJV) – "There is a way *that seems* right to a man, but its end *is* the way of death."

1 Peter 2:4-10
Romans 9
Psalm 16:7-11
Proverbs 12:28
Proverbs 2
Jeremiah 6:16-19
Genesis 3:8-10

The Token

The token of My affection
Leads you in a different direction
The Holy Spirit is His name
Changing lives is His fame

What does this token cost?
To those whose lives are broken, lost?
I've already paid the price
The Lamb - a perfect sacrifice

Just ask for this token so rare
It is given freely if you dare
Come place all your trust in Me
Step out in faith and let Me lead

My sacrifice was worth the cost
I'd pay if only one was lost
Yes, you mean that much to Me
I want to be with you eternally

Just hold out your hand to Me
Receive this token, My pledge to thee
Let Him come live within your heart
He'll never leave you or depart

July 22, 2016

Token – 1. Something serving to indicate some fact, feeling, event, etc.; mark or sign. 2. Sign of friendship, keepsake. 3. Piece of metal stamped for a higher value than the metal is worth. 4. Piece of metal indicating a right or privilege. 5. Something that is a sign of genuineness or authority. 6. As a token of; to show. 7. Serving as a symbol; nominal; partial. 8. Symbol, indication, memento, memorial. Taken from Thorndike Barnhart Comprehensive desk Dictionary.

Exodus 12:12-13 KJV – "For I will pass through the land of Egypt this night, and will smite all the firstborn in the land of Egypt, both man and beast; and against all the gods of Egypt I will execute judgment: I am the LORD.
¹³ And the blood shall be to you for a token upon the houses where ye are: and when I see the blood, I will pass over you, and the plague shall not be upon you to destroy you, when I smite the land of Egypt."

Romans 5:14-21
Acts 2:38-39
Acts 19:1-7
Matthew 3:11
Ephesians 1:11-14
Hebrews 13:5
Deuteronomy 31:6

The Train Whistle

The train whistle's calling me "Come away, hurry!"
Day is far spent, my past is all blurry
Engrossing my thoughts is my future a calling
My heart skips a beat with a wistful longing

For off in the distance, a way do I see
A path in the wilderness, prepared just for me
Looking down at my feet, a footprint I spy
And raising my face, I catch my Lord's eye

The love on His face catches my breath
I will follow Him anywhere, even to death
There is no other path, no other way
Than to follow His footsteps day by day

At the end of life's journey, my Lord will be there
As He was by my side in life's journey's frontier
We will dance at our wedding, our joy complete
Together, forever, at His mercy seat

Friday, August 5, 2011

Philippians 3:12-21
Ephesians 2:6-10
Song of Solomon 2:10,13
Revelation 19:6-9
Ephesians 5:31-33

On that warm summer morning, looking out the bedroom window down into the garden, I told my husband, Harvey, that I would be down shortly to help him after finishing a chore I had started. Just then, far in the distance over the still dew filled air, a long train whistle sounded out, and it seemed to be calling to me. How strange, I thought, that this haunting call seemed to be telling me a message. I listened more intently, and yes, it was trying to tell me something.

"Come away with me, come away with me", the faint chugging engine sounded out. A wistful longing filled me and I replied in my heart, "I can't come with you, my husband doesn't like to travel, and my place is here. This is where I need to be". I felt a poem from the Lord, coming into my thoughts, and I sat down to write it out, before the feeling faded away.

Within a year, Harvey died from a sudden heart attack. In the wilderness of grief and loneliness, I sensed a pathway before me, directing me, and showing me the way I must go. The Lord was so faithful to me during this time.

Prayer: Yes, Lord, I will arise and follow You.

Grief's Journey

Beside the still waters I rest my soul
My grief is heavy, it has taken a toll
The lamp does flicker, it grows ever dim
A life is cut short, why did it have to be him?

Beauty for ashes, I can't wait to see
How can God use this to benefit me?
But faith will arise and turn into sight
As it becomes real and reaches new heights

God is the same and ever will be
He will cut loose cords that now restrict me
As I grow to new heights in the field of life
The darkness recedes in the dawn's new light

A way in the wilderness, cut just for me
Following Him closely, a way do I see
It leads upward and onward, till I reach heaven's door
When I cross the threshold, joy evermore

July 10, 2012

Psalm 23
Isaiah 61:1-3
Revelation 4:1

Water Song

Dancing, splashing flowing free
Waters' song calls out to me
What is it saying? I listen close
"Immerse yourself in Me from your head to your toes"

The river of life flows out of God's throne
To water the harvest and the seeds sown
This circle of life will then be complete
When all are gathered at the mercy seat

If anyone is thirsty let him come drink of Me
It releases My Spirit deep within thee
Outward it flows, giving life to all
Refreshing creation both the great and the small

The Spirit and the bride say, "come"
It is only by His Spirit that we overcome
"Immerse yourself in Me from your head to your toes"
You will be carried along where ever this river flows

July 24, 2016

John 7:37-39
Revelation 22:1-5
John 4:10-15
Revelation 21:6-7
Isaiah 55
Revelation 22:17

I was enjoying listening to my small splashing fountain outside my open window one summer night while praying in my bedroom. It was almost as if the water was playing a song. I listened closer to hear what the happy melody was singing and this poem came to me.

Waters' circle of life goes from mist to rain to bodies of water and back to water vapor again. So it is with our spirits. God breathes life into our bodies at conception and we become a living spirit/body. We live as spirit/bodies of water on earth and return to only spirit at the end to rise and return to God. It is called the circle of life.

In the scripture verses listed we see both the Word (Jesus) and the Holy Spirit being compared to water. They are always calling to us during our lifetime to be conscious of Them and invite Them into our lives daily to communicate with Them.

Ask Them for direction; ask Them for love, grace, and mercy and you will hear Their reply in many different ways. Throughout our life They are always calling to us, sometimes in song. Answer Them.

Vision of the Pillar of Cloud

A pillar of cloud, smoke, fire and wind
Appeared southeast in the sky suspended
Beneath it four horses with riders they flew
Like a chariot racing across the sky's blue

In a flash above me, the swirling cloud stood
It seemed to wait for me I understood
Watching from above as I traveled the path
Directing my way through the battle scarred swath

Like the ones in the desert, the fire lighted my way
Turning the cold night into warm day
During hot days, the smoke shaded the sun
Providing relief and shade till the battle was won

What is the meaning of this I wondered?
In His watch over me the Lord did not slumber
Providing for me every step of the way
Was my guardian, helper, provider and stay

What an honor is this, my heart did fear
That the Creator of the universe over me would appear
And light my path from heaven above
To shower me with His mercy and love!

Then I realized what the gap in time meant
The Lord would always be with me wherever I was sent
From the swirling dark pillar came the eye of the Lord
Watching everything taking place as He traveled the world

June 14 2014

Deuteronomy 33:26 -29- "There is no one like the God of Jeshurun who rides across the heavens to help you and on the clouds in his majesty. [27] The eternal God is your refuge, and underneath are the everlasting arms. He will drive out your enemies before you, saying, 'Destroy them!'
[28] So Israel will live in safety; Jacob will dwell secure in a land of grain and new wine, where the heavens drop dew. [29] Blessed are you, Israel! Who is like you, a people saved by the Lord? He is your shield and helper and your glorious sword. Your enemies will cower before you, and you will tread on their heights."

2 Chronicles 16:9 – "For the eyes of the Lord range throughout the earth to strengthen those whose hearts are fully committed to him."

Psalm 68:1-17, 32-35
Psalm 18:6-19

A while ago, I received a vision from the Lord. In part of the vision, I saw a pillar of cloud coming toward me rapidly with four horses under it with riders. I didn't see the riders clearly because I was focused on the fast approaching whirlwind. The cloud was dark, and swirling with fire and lightening inside of it. Somehow, I knew the Lord's eye was watching from inside. This swirling pillar stopped above me, watching me as I drove in my car below. I seemed to be watching this from above. I couldn't figure out why this cloud stood above me and there seemed to be a gap in time until the scene shifted to something else in the vision. What did this mean? I pondered it for months.

In my prayer time one morning, I asked the Lord the meaning. I received this poem as my answer.

Prayer: Your ways Lord, are far above ours. Your power and majesty are a wonder to behold. But it is Your love for us that is the biggest mystery. That You would stoop to look down at Your humble creation to provide and care for us is what we will marvel forever.

Chapter 5
Redemption

The New Birth

"It is finished", came the cry
Arms outstretched, He bled and died
Look on Him who paid your sin
The curtain's torn, the graves are opened

An earthquake rents the deep dark earth
A way is opened, a second birth
Just as flesh is torn the first time round
A new man emerges from the ground

From dust to dust He came to die
Ours is not to question why
The perfect God should pay the price
For us to enter paradise

April 2, 2014

Matthew 27:50-54
Luke 23:42-49
Hebrews 10:19-23

On a gloomy Lenten morning, I was picturing Christ hanging on a blood stained cross. You could almost sense the darkness gathering, a storm approaching. The temple sacrifices were taking place across the hill from where He hung, and Passover lambs were being slain. After the last lamb was slaughtered the High Priest would have raised his outstretched arms and declared "It is finished". It would have been about the same time, late afternoon that Christ, His arms outstretched on the cross, uttered those same words. The earthquake that followed, caused the temple curtain to be torn in two, symbolizing, a way was opening for us into the holy of holies. As I finished this poem, the sun broke out, immersing me in warm sunlight, a picture of the resurrection.

Prayer: Thank you, Lord, for dying for my sins. Let me never lose the wonder, the amazement of the price You had to pay to do that. We pray for our loved ones and the ones who don't know You as Savior and Lord, to have their eyes opened to the fact that You died for them also. We pray this message would go around the world to every person and nation.

God of glory, Lord of love
Praise to You who reigns above
Showering us with love and favor
From Your Son, redeeming Savior

The Victorious Lamb

Before time existed, a plan was laid
From the foundation of the earth, a Lamb should be slain
A holy nation was decreed to arise
Praise to our Creator would soon fill the skies

Worthy, worthy is the Lamb
Look! Caught in the dense thicket, behold a Ram!
A God-sent sacrifice in place of Abraham's son
Obedience displayed, the victory won

On Calvary's hill the plan did unfold
In every nation and tribe the story was told
Now, forever, in heaven our story will be
Praise to the Lamb whose blood set us free!

Refrain

Oh Lamb that was slain
From the foundation of the earth
The Lamb took my place
And gave me new birth

Friday, June 29, 2012

Genesis 22
Ephesians 1:4
Hebrews 10

The Lion and the Lamb

Who can glory in the presence of the Lamb?
Jesus is our King, the great "I AM"
He raises the lowly from the dust of the earth
And offers them salvation, a second birth

Worthy are You to take the scroll
To open its seals to discover its goals
For with Your blood You purchased men
From every tribe, language and nation

See the Lion majestic and fierce
Appear as a Lamb who had been pierced
Standing in the center of the throne on high
Possessing seven horns and having seven eyes

As heaven paused to take in this picture
The Lamb stepped forward as a mighty victor
Taking the scroll from Him on the throne
Caused all in heaven to worship and fall prone

Worthy is the Lamb who was beaten and then slain
Who endured the cross and suffered great shame
But now will reign forever and ever
With His bride by His side rejoicing together

July 13, 2015

Revelation 5

Who can presume position or glory in His presence? As I was meditating on Revelation 5 one morning this poem came to me. What a scene in heaven this describes! The King of Kings is getting ready to return to earth to slay His enemies and take back what was taken from Adam.

Through the trials of life we can be sure of the end of the story. It is a tale of victory.

Prayer: You are too wonderful and majestic for words to express. We cannot even fathom what You had to go through to redeem men back to You. Eternal praise is not enough. Help me to live my life as an offering pleasing to You. Show me Your ways so that I may not sin against You.

One Special Day

In the stillness of the beauteous night
Arises One with rapturous light
Up from the dust of the lowly earth
Emerges a King of noble birth

The angels praise the Lord on High
As galaxies dance in the cold night sky
The shepherds stand transfixed in fear
While lowly sheep are resting near

Not many notice, not many see
A sacrifice prepared for me
Disguised in human form He came
To live, to love, to bear the blame

My blessed One, who died for me
And opened the gates of eternity
Now humbles Himself to enter my heart
I praise you, I praise you, my Savior Thou art

December 23, 2010

Luke 2:1-20
Hebrews 10:5-10

What an amazing story, that the Creator of the universe came to our planet for the purpose of being a sacrifice for the sins of the human race! The gifts the magi brought Him were prophetic of His mission; gold for the King of Kings, myrrh for His death as a sacrifice for sin, and frankincense as the future High Priest who ever intercedes for us.

And not only that, He waits humbly at the door of our heart before we choose to let Him in, or in some cases He is still refused entrance.

Prayer: Let us never lose the wonder of the Christmas message. In this festive season, let us decorate the walls of our hearts with praise, and let our eyes reflect the love of Jesus, as our hands prepare to do His work.

The Eagle Has Landed

An eagles' first flight is fraught with danger
Look! In Bethlehem, see a babe in a manger
Dressed in swaddling clothes, with straw as a nest
A perfect lamb came down, heaven sent its best

The enemy came to seek and destroy
Herod sent soldiers to kill the small boy
The parents took flight and went down to Egypt
The wings of the Father protected the small eaglet

As the baby boy grew, filled with truth and grace
He departed the nest and sought His Father's face
This led Him into danger and untold stories
As He showed the Father's love and manifest glories

See the Father's love, how great beyond measure
Portrayed by His Son, a priceless treasure
Now ascended on high, He is seated above
But sent down His Spirit in the form of a dove

He will return one day, to gather His bride
To be with Him forever, a queen by His side
We will reign forever in the skies above
Revealing His majesty, grace, truth and love

May 7, 2014

Deuteronomy 32:10-14
Exodus 19:3-4
Isaiah 40:28-31

    The past few months, I have been captivated watching the web cam of an eagles' nest in the Hays section of Pittsburgh. Three eaglets emerged from their eggs looking like dryer lint and so helpless. It was so thrilling to see the devoted majestic looking parents caring for them. The birds grew quickly under their parents watchful eyes. I looked up the many verses in the bible about eagles, and saw a comparison was made about God and His people. Jesus, our brother, became as helpless as we are, and submitted to His Father. He is our example.

Just this morning, I watched the web site of another eagles' first flight in Florida under the watchful eyes of its parents. Mom and dad flew around the fledgling bird showing him how it was done and verbally encouraging him to try it.

Filled with wonder by this, I got the first line of this poem. When I got the second line, I had no idea where this poem was going, as usual. As I wrote the rest of this poem, I sensed the Father's love and care for us. How He longs to shelter and provide for us under His wings. Let Him. Don't be like Jerusalem.

Matthew 23:37-39 – "Jerusalem, Jerusalem, you who kill the prophets and stone those sent to you, how often I have longed to gather your children together, as a hen gathers her chicks under her wings, and you were not willing.

Prayer: We are willing, Lord, to follow You, to leave our safe nest. Thank You for sending us, Jesus, to show the way, to be our example. We do want to follow Your Spirit wherever He may lead us.

Psalm 139:9,10 – "If I rise on the wings of the dawn, if I settle on the far side of the sea, 10 even there your hand will guide me, your right hand will hold me fast."

Bought With a Price

I'm covered, I'm covered by the blood of the Lamb
Sealed by a covenant with the great "I AM"
For with His blood He purchased the lost
Redemption has come at a very high cost

Do not treat it lightly and live as you please
For each stripe I bore has healed sins' disease
You are bought with a price from off the slave block
Abide close to Me so your shackles I can unlock

My love is a river it flows deep and wide
It casts out all fear when you enter its tide
Wash yourself in the waters of the Word
Be ye doers of all that is heard

A new world is coming and I will dwell among men
With those under covenant who were faithful till the end
For they are worthy and will be dressed in white
They will dwell in My city and partake its delights

November 29, 2016

Romans 6
Hosea 3:1-3
Psalm 36:5-10
Psalm 46:1-4
James 1:19-27
Revelation 19:5-9
Revelation 21

Uninvited Guest at the Last Supper

Let no one say, "I am tempted of the Lord"
It is by our own sin we are bound with a cord
As Judas was tempted with silver and fame
Not perceiving it led to his destruction and shame

At the Passover dinner, on that intimate night
An intruder came, but was hidden from sight
He asked of the Lord to sift Simon as wheat
But because Jesus prayed, it did not remain a defeat

Satan then turned to the others at the table
Releasing his pride, the night's plans to disable
A dispute arose amongst those who were there
Of who would be greatest, their fame to declare

"How easy", thought Satan, a smile crossed his face
His trap was now set, everything in place
He entered into Judas to carry out his plan
To rid his domain of Jesus, the man

As Judas hurried out into the cool night air
His thoughts of gain would soon turn to despair
For the Potter who made him, Himself became clay
Betrayed by his hand, He would die the next day

Wonder of wonders that our Savior would die
To purchase our pardon, our Redeemer drew nigh
Thirty pieces of silver, the value placed on Him
He redeemed the Potter's field and all that's therein

April 11, 2014

James 1:13-15
Luke 22:1-34
John 13:1-28
Matthew 27:1-10

    As I sat reading and thinking about the Last Supper one day in Lent, the Lord brought to my mind's eye, another person who came into the room on that intimate night. The old master's paintings usually only show 13 present, but there were 14 gathered there. One slipped in unawares by the 12, but noticed by Jesus. Is that when Satan asked Jesus to sift Peter as wheat?

    When darkness himself came into the room to enter Judas, did he pause first to cause further damage by releasing pride into those gathered there? Did this darkness cause humility to flee as the disciples started jockeying for position on who would be greatest?

At dinner that night, Jesus had just washed their feet, a picture of humility and serving, giving them an example of their future mission. But Jesus took this conflict and used it as a teaching moment.

It wasn't until Jesus gave Judas permission to betray Him that the plan was able to go forward. Angels were restrained from protecting Jesus after that point in time.

If God is the master Potter in Jeremiah 18, the Potters field could prophetically be the whole earth in the passion story. Jesus' blood not only redeems us, but also the whole earth will be redeemed on that Day. (Romans 8:18-25)

Prayer: Protect me Lord, from the enemy's plans. Help me to draw so close to You that I choose You over disobedience and material things. I draw the cloak of humility over me to protect me from desiring to be noticed and admired. I invite You to come and eat with me and have communion with those of like mind. I pray for me and Your church to be overcomers.

John 11:49-52 – "⁴⁹ Then one of them, named Caiaphas, who was high priest that year, spoke up, "You know nothing at all! ⁵⁰ You do not realize that it is better for you that one man die for the people than that the whole nation perish." ⁵¹ He did not say this on his own, but as high priest that year he prophesied that Jesus would die for the Jewish nation, ⁵² and not only for that nation but also for the scattered children of God, to bring them together and make them one."

High Priest of Heaven

High Priest of heaven interceding for me
Who set me apart and marked me as holy
The sacrifice of blood required by law
Was paid in full by His death at Golgatha

The Light of the world stands in the holy place
His eyes are aflame, glory shines from His face
His feet are on fire but are not consumed
While His pure white robe emits a fragrant perfume

In His hand the showbread is offered to me
Bread of heaven came down and died at Calvary
Now in remembrance this bread we do eat
Till we see Him again and in heaven do meet

At the table of incense He waits for our prayers
Smoke rises to heaven and the Father hears
He sends out the angels to perform His will
As we wait in faith, humble, praying and still

In the Holy of Holies the curtain was torn
As the Savior hung dying with a crown of thorns
With His arms open wide, love and mercy did meet
Granting us access to the mercy seat

Three days later the grave could not hold Him
The doors of Sheol suddenly burst open
In the garden He arose with victory over death
Reclaiming the garden in which Adam lost his breath

Now in heaven He is seated on high
The Lion of Judah resembling a Lamb that had died
The High Priest of heaven is waiting for me
Behold His arms open wide with love and mercy

October 18, 2014

Hebrews 7:23-28
Hebrews 8
Hebrews 9
Hebrews 10:19-23
Revelation 1:12-18
Revelation 5:5-14

    I awoke in the middle of the night. As I started praying, I sensed I was in the Lord's presence. Even though I didn't see anything with my natural eyes, I knew somehow that I was in the Holy Place in the temple and Jesus was nearby dressed as the High Priest in a white robe standing by the Menorah. He was offering something to me. I couldn't see Him clearly, but I knew it was Him.

    Then, I got the first sentence of this poem and got out of bed to write it down, knowing I would be getting more verses.

    In the Old Testament times, priests ministered daily in the Holy Place at the temple at Jerusalem. In this room was the Menorah (branched candlestick), table of showbread, and the table of incense. In chapters 7,

8 and 9 in Hebrews, we see Jesus as our High Priest of a new covenant ministering in the heavenly temple.

This poem beautifully shows how Jesus fulfills the ritual that the earthly priest once performed daily. He is the High Priest of Heaven interceding for us.

Hebrews 7:23-25 – "Now there have been many of those priests, since death prevented them from continuing in office; *24* *but because Jesus lives forever, he has a permanent priesthood.* *25* *Therefore he is able to save completely those who come to God through him, because he always lives to intercede for them."*

Prayer: High Priest of Heaven, You not only see everything that takes place on earth, but also You see into the hearts of men. Forgive my sins and cleanse me. You are waiting for us to come into Your presence through prayer. We are not worthy except by Your blood that You shed for us. Let us not delay or make You wait.

Hebrews 8:1-2 – "Now the main point of what we are saying is this: We do have such a high priest, who sat down at the right hand of the throne of the Majesty in heaven, *2* *and who serves in the sanctuary, the true tabernacle set up by the Lord, not by a mere human being."*

My Grateful Heart

How can I begin to show my grateful heart?
For all of the blessings into my life You impart
You are close by, even when I'm not aware
It is in the small details that I see how You care

We were by nature objects of great wrath
When we followed dark spirits down disobedient paths
Because of Your great love You set us free
And willfully took our place on Calvary's tree

You are working in me what is pleasing to You
As I put off the old self and put on the new
Teach me Your ways, bring me into the light
In the blood of the Lamb, wash my robe white

In heavenly places You are seated on high
And You raise us up and invite us to draw nigh
In the coming ages we'll see the riches of Your grace
The best part of all, we'll see You face to face

October 13, 2016

Ephesians 2:1-10
Hebrews 11:20-21
Ephesians 4:22-24
Ephesians 5:8-14
Revelation 7:14

Eden Restored

With joy draw water from the well of salvation
For you were His from the dawn of creation
The crowning achievement is earthly man's story
Made from the dust, but reflecting God's glory

Given dominion on the earth to rule
Walking with God in the evening cool
Seeking God's face in friendship sweet
Heaven came down in Eden to meet

Deception crept in followed by sin and death
Stealing Adam's authority and even his breath
The terrible cost that disobedience earned
Relief from the curse what creation yearned

The "Son of Man" came to seek what was lost
Enduring rejection and paying the cost
On a faraway hill the price was paid
With His arms opened wide, the "Way" was laid

Debbie Furey

He is the Way, the Truth and the Life
Our Bridegroom, the Lord, came seeking a wife
One day He'll return and gather His bride
Together, forever, we will reign by His side

The redeemed creation will surpass the first
God's mercy extended to even the worst
Love so amazing will be revealed
The heavens restored, humanity sealed

August 11, 2014

Genesis 2 & 3
Romans 8:18-25
Ephesians 1:3-23
Psalm 8

When we think of the Lord's second coming, we don't always think about Eden being restored, but that is exactly what will happen. The focus on the return of Christ is usually the battle over the earth and the judgments taking place, and that will happen first. But, we know the whole story and the end of the book. So we can look forward with joy to His return for us.

Prayer: Your glory will be revealed to the whole earth at Your return, Lord. Not only will our bodies be redeemed, but creation will be redeemed also. Once again, man will walk in the garden with You. Eden will be restored.

Chapter 6
Holy Fire

Holy Fire

God of glory, my desire
Purify me with holy fire
Drawn from heaven's altar's flames,
Touch my heart, my life, my frame

Draw me with Your sweet perfume
Till in love I am consumed
Light my path and help me see
Holy footprints leading me

Upward, onward, a rocky way
Your presence turns my night to day
Till at last I see Your face
Brought there safely by Your grace

There forever I will be
Refined by fire for all to see
A gem reflecting all Your glory
Telling of my life, my story

December, 2013

Isaiah 6:1-7
Song of Solomon 1:3
Malachi 3:1-4, 16-18

A Yielded Heart

A yielded heart is my desire
One that responds to Holy Spirit's fire
Purging out the will to sin
Receiving peace from deep within

A purifying fire does burn
Testing motives and heartfelt yearns
I surrender daily to His will
My deepest desires He will fulfill

A yielded heart is His desire
He comes to baptize me with fire
His winnowing fork is in His hand
To sift out hearts that understand

May 28, 2017

Luke 12:49 – "I have come to bring fire on the earth, and how I wish it were already kindled!"

Malachi 3:1-4
Psalm 37:3-6
Matthew 3:11-12
Matthew 13: 10-17

Definition of winnow – to free as grain from chaff, by means of wind or driven air

The Holy Spirit is portrayed as a mighty rushing wind in the book of Acts. When you winnow at harvest, the fork throws the grain into the air. It's not really the fork that sifts us it's the wind.

The Burning Bride

Oh holy fire that burns so bright
Consume my soul and give me sight
Burn away what holds me back
Impart the gifts I sorely lack

Three Hebrews in the fire were bound
Licking flames - the ropes unwound
Eyes were opened and one could see
The Son of God walking among the three

Tongues of fire on Pentecost fell
Gifts were released as Jesus did foretell
The Holy Spirit came and dwelt in their hearts
Strength and courage did the flames impart

As the wise virgins gathered oil for their lamps
The fire of God fell and was invited to encamp
This caused the wise ones to make their dress white
Consuming her dross, imparting grace and sight

Come holy fire that dwells at God's throne
The seven fold Spirit that forms the Corner-stone
Come down upon me and burn all the dross
As I lay down my will and take up Your cross

March 28, 2016

Daniel 3
Acts 2
Matthew 25:1-13
Revelation 4:5
Ephesians 2:19-22
1 Peter 2:4-12
Matthew 16:24-27

Holy, Holy, Holy

I long to see Your beauty as it says in Your Word
You are high and lifted up in the courts of the Lord
Your servants stand in awe at the throne room on high
Holy, holy, holy is the seraphs loud cry

Before Your throne there are seven lamps blazing
Causing sights and sounds to reveal the amazing
The door posts shake at the sound of Your voice
As Your judgments come forth causing saints to rejoice

In the center, around the throne, are four living creatures
They are covered with eyes yet have distinct features
Each has six wings with which to fly
Holy, holy, holy is the creature's loud cry

The victorious were standing beside the sea of glass
Watching seven angels carry seven plagues as they passed
They sang the song of Moses and the song of the Lamb
For You alone are holy and the great "I Am"

They sang, "True and just are Your judgments oh Lord"
As the angels tipped bowls and the wrath was outpoured
Flashes of lightning and mighty peals of thunder
Caused the earth to quake and the mountains split asunder

Heaven stood open as the Lord came down
His eyes were blazing and on His head were many crowns
He is coming to rule, behold, a new age will appear
Holy, holy, holy cries the earth as He draws near

February 6, 2016

Psalm 27:4
Isaiah 6:1-4
Revelation chapters 4, 15, 16, and 19
Romans 8:19-23

Mercy, Mercy

Angels in the starry heights
Behold the Lord with veiled sight
Waves of glory around them rise
Causing praise to fill the skies

Holy, holy is the cry
Mercy, mercy my reply
God is love, I know it's true
Causing hope to spring anew

But also know He judges sin
In His presence we must begin
To lay down every sinful way
Plead His blood, my sins to pay

Fear the Lord, let wisdom rise
Causing praise to fill the skies
Holy, holy is the cry
Mercy, mercy my reply

Thursday December 19, 2013

Isaiah 6:1-7
Revelation 4:2-11
1 Peter 4:17-19
2 Peter 2:20-22

I got this poem one morning while trying to imagine what the Lord looked like. Isaiah 6 records what he saw and his reaction. It was a fearsome thing in the Old Testament when anyone saw a vision of the Lord. The pureness and holiness of God exposes the sin nature of our heart. Our natural response is to ask for mercy. The other response is to worship in awe. What a sight awaits us in heaven!

Prayer: As we come into Your presence, Lord, forgive our sins. We thank You for the shed blood of Jesus who took our sin upon Himself so that we may be righteous in Your sight. The fear of the Lord is the beginning of wisdom, so I pray we never trample or presume upon Your mercy and grace. Teach us to be holy in all we do.

The Master Potter

As earthly clay is baked by fire
To create an object of the potter's desire
So you are in My loving hands
To walk in love and the law's demands

Your place, your value, is determined by Me
The design imprinted is for all to see
For a special purpose you were created
In space and time your existence was dated

The potter's field is the whole earth
It belongs to Me and has tremendous worth
For it was redeemed by the Savior's blood
Purified by fire and a cleansing flood

Soon I will come to reclaim what is Mine
To take back what was stolen by the enemies design
Those that oppose will be slain by Me
Out of My mouth comes a sword to strike down My enemy

I will return to reign on the earth
With a queen by My side of immeasurable worth
Together forever we will reign on high
My beloved, My bride, the apple of My eye

Debbie Furey

December 22, 2014

Jeremiah 18:1-10
Zechariah 11:12-13
Matthew 27:1-10
2 Peter 3:5-7
Romans 9:14-24
Revelation 19:11-16

We do not usually think of God in this context, but scripture clearly portrays Him as a master potter. He makes vessels as He chooses, not as we would wish and each vessel is made with a purpose in mind. Our life's goal is to find that purpose and pursue it with all our strength. We can waste our life, but it comes at great peril, and we will have to give an account of the talents we were given.

Prayer: Let my life be lived in Your will and for Your pleasure. Help me to keep my eyes on You and stay on the path of life. Help me to fulfill my destiny.

Chapter 7
Still Speaking

Still Speaking

The holy men of God still speak
On pages stained with blood and ink
With some their blood cries from the ground
Heaven still echoes with its sound

From battlefields or sacred throngs
These men to God alone belonged
They loved the Lord more than their breath
The cross was theirs even unto death

They walked with pilgrim feet to seek
A better country where dwelt the meek
A place whose builder and maker is God
A heavenly city where angels trod

By faith they conquered in God's name
Accepting torture, jeers and shame
The worlds not worthy of these men
Who wandered in deserts and dark dens

Now with God they are seated on high
As kings and priests as the ages roll by
Together with us we will be complete
With God as our head at the mercy seat

July 4, 2016

Matthew 23:29-39
Hebrews 11
Ephesians 1:15-23

Able's Blood Still Speaks

Able's blood still cries from the ground
It talks to us though we can't hear a sound
Come closer, listen, you will hear it speak
"Justice, justice", is its terrible shriek

A life cut short that would have resulted in many
The value of his life was reduced to a penny
Dust returns to dust, but the soul lives on
Only heaven or hell are the choices beyond

The death of the righteous is precious in God's sight
They are ushered to His presence at the speed of light
There they are rewarded and given robes of white
And then told to wait until all things are made right

Don't be like Cain who belonged to the evil one
He lied then the Lord asked him, "What have you done"?
His brother's blood was crying out loud
So the Lord cursed Cain and the ground he had plowed

Blood is the sacrifice required by the Lord
It was shown from the beginning and cannot be ignored
Jesus our Savior, the perfect sinless Lamb
Took our place, slain on our behalf, He is the great "I AM"

April 6, 2017

Genesis 4:1-12
Hebrews 11:4
Revelation 6:9-11
1 John 3:12
Hebrews 9 & 10

Cain and Able obviously knew a blood sacrifice was required by the Lord, but Cain willfully chose another offering. In Genesis 4:6-7, the Lord speaks to Cain and reminded him what he needed to do to be accepted. Cain refused.

From the beginning, blood being shed to cover sin was the pattern. Cain's parents, Adam and Eve, tried to cover themselves with fig leaves after they sinned and saw that they were naked before God. This was not acceptable to God and the Lord made garments of animal skin for Adam and Eve and clothed them. An animal had to be slain to do that. Was this when God revealed to them the need for a blood sacrifice?

Since the fall of Adam and Eve we see a blood sacrifice being the pattern of acceptance in God's sight in the Bible. It is the blood that covers our sins. Animal sacrifices were the picture of the perfect sacrifice that was to come – Jesus, the Lamb of God. Hebrews 9 & 10 detail how Jesus took upon Himself the curse of sin in our place. If we believe this and repent of our sin, then we are saved.

Be Like Ruth

Watch and see My servant Ruth
Set in her story, are many truths
Of My fervent love and holy grace
Come, My child, take her place

Come and drink My grace divine
Come and eat, all I have is thine
Reach out in faith and seek My face
Desire My presence, take her place

No weapon formed against thee
Will ever harm or separate ye
From My endless love and healing balm
Reach out, come closer, rest under My arm

Follow close, at last, we will reach heaven's door
Where we will be together, forever more
You will share My throne in My kingdom above
Come, take Ruth's place and accept my love

February 1, 2014

The book of Ruth

I received this poem because of a request I made to the Lord. I had started a neighborhood bible study to get to know my neighbors better. Picking the book of Ruth, we not only looked at the story line, but also how it was a picture or type of the Christians' walk. The story is a progression of someone getting to know the Lord, then the preparation of getting ready for our Bridegroom, and ending with fulfillment of a destiny. Its' teaching goes far beyond just a romantic love story.

One morning as I was praying for the ladies in the bible study, I asked the Lord for a poem to give them from Him. This is the answer to that request.

Prayer: What a privilege, Lord, to get this invitation from You. This beckoning is on every page of the bible. Let us respond with a joyful heart and praise on our lips to Your love for us. What a destiny awaits us!

Alive By Faith

When the Lord asked Ezekiel, "Can these bones live"?
Was He looking for an answer to a puzzling quiz?
When the Lord asks a question, does He not know?
It's faith He is searching for in those here below

Of course, bones can't live, what could be more dead?
"Lord, You alone know", said the prophet instead
"Speak life to those bones", said the Lord in reply
So the prophet was obedient to the Lord's clear cry

In response to his faith, the bones started quaking
And they came together with a terrible shaking
What a fearsome sight to see death come alive
In the newly formed bodies God's breath did revive

This vast new army is the house of Israel
To their land I'll bring them strong and invincible
My people will know then that I am the Lord
My Spirit within them in their hand My sword

In this newly formed nation there will be one King
Israel returned to their land My praises will sing
They will be My people and I will be their God
Reclaiming the land where Joshua once trod

Can a country be born in a day?
Ask Isaiah and see what he will say
When the fullness of the Gentiles will come to an end
The natural branches will be grafted back in

The new olive tree will then be complete
Jew and Gentile together in harmony sweet
One new man who once was two
Will worship together in Spirit and in truth

November 10, 2014

Ezekiel 37
Isaiah 66:7-13
Romans 11
Ephesians 2:11-22
Ephesians 3:2-6
Joshua 1:3
Jeremiah 31:31-40

I awoke this morning a little after 4:00 AM and couldn't go back to sleep. My mind drifted to Ezekiel 37 and Isaiah 66. They are both about the nation of Israel becoming a nation again after many years of being dispersed throughout the world. Both of these scriptures were fulfilled on May 14, 1948. The dead bones came to life and became a nation in a day and are now a mighty army.

I got the first two lines of this poem and arose to write them down. In a few hours the poem was done.

It was interesting how often in the past few days; the theme of Israel and Gentiles being united in the future came to my mind. I had been asking the Lord what was on His heart and mind. I feel this poem is an answer to that question.

Prayer: Lord, You said to pray for the peace of Jerusalem and I pray for that now. I also pray that the Prince of Peace would come soon and establish His kingdom on earth. May the church and Israel be one in harmony and unity.

John 11:49-52 – "Then one of them, named Caiaphas, who was high priest that year, spoke up, "You know nothing at all! [50] You do not realize that it is better for you that one man die for the people than that the whole nation perish."
[51] He did not say this on his own, but as high priest that year he prophesied that Jesus would die for the Jewish nation, [52] and not only for that nation

but also for the scattered children of God, to bring them together and make them one."

Romans 11:25-27 – "[25] *I do not want you to be ignorant of this mystery, brothers and sisters, so that you may not be conceited: Israel has experienced a hardening in part until the full number of the Gentiles has come in,* [26] *and in this way all Israel will be saved. As it is written:*
"The deliverer will come from Zion;
he will turn godlessness away from Jacob.
27 And this is my covenant with them
when I take away their sins."

Esther's Song

Oh to see through the swirling mist of time
The beauty of Esther, displaying grace so sublime
The plot was so intricate, only God could devise
A victory so complete, bringing her enemies demise

Would I see her dancing through time's swirling mist?
In intimacy with You while her enemies persist
She fasted and prayed as You worked behind the scene
To protect and defend Your chosen precious queen

The swirling mist of time cannot erase the story
Of You protecting Israel and displaying Your mighty glory
For You are the King over the whole earth
We will have eternity to declare Your beauty and worth

Faint strains reach my ears of Esther's sweet song
As she sings it in glory amongst heaven's throng
The melodious tune declares God's faithfulness
And everlasting love that proves measureless

February 4, 2017

Esther 4:15 – "[15] Then Esther sent this reply to Mordecai: [16] "Go, gather together all the Jews who are in Susa, and fast for me. Do not eat or drink for three days, night or day. I and my attendants will fast as you do. When this is done, I will go to the king, even though it is against the law. And if I perish, I perish."

Esther 3, 4, 5, 6, 7, 8

Two Thieves on a Cross

One thief on the cross is eternally lost
The decision he made came at great cost
His foolish eyes had been darkened by sin
The trial he was going through produced no change within

He attacked his only hope as he jeered with the crowd
Looking not at himself, his heart remained proud
Years of rebellion had turned his heart to stone
In the flames of hell he will eternally groan

The other thief repented and Jesus forgave
His eyes beheld the Lamb, came from heaven to save
Sorrow for his sin produced a change within
The fear of the Lord opened his eyes to his sin

He had attacked his only hope as he jeered with the crowd
Then changed his mind as he wondered aloud
This thief was punished justly, but our Savior did no wrong
When Jesus went to paradise He took him along

Two robbers were crucified, one on each side
One is in hell, the other in heaven resides
Which one will you be as you stop to compare?
One thief was saved so we need not despair

Two thieves on a cross at the end of the story
Only one went to heaven with Jesus in glory
Fear the Lord, for we are under the same sentence
The only way there is through faith and repentance

March 29, 2017

Matthew 27:38-44
Luke 23:32-43

1 Corinthians 1:18 – "For the message of the cross is foolishness to those who are perishing, but to us who are being saved it is the power of God."

I heard a saying once: One thief was saved so we need not despair, but only one so that we do not presume.

One might be tempted to think we can get to heaven if our good deeds out-weigh our bad deeds. But how many good deeds do we need to do if this is our belief? How many wrongs bring us over the line to where it keeps us out of heaven?

If we truly believe this, we are telling Jesus, who came to die for our sins, that we would rather trust in getting ourselves to heaven. This would render His sacrifice as not enough, or incomplete.

He came to take our place so that we are saved from the judgment of our sins. Jesus declares Himself the way, the truth and the life in John 14:6. No one comes to the Father except through Him.

We must have faith to believe this and repent and turn from our sins.

Chapter 8
Our Reward

Our Reward

Search not here for your reward
For it is up in heaven stored
There it waits, it tells your story
Of how you gave the Lord the glory

The treasure reflects a hidden life
Of love, of giving, of sacrifice
There is nothing on earth that can compare
For what's in store for us up there

But, best of all, we'll see the Father's face
As we stand before Him, in that hallowed place
We'll hear the words "Well done, My son"
Come sit with Me, the battle's won

Then we'll enter heaven's glory
Our crown reflecting each our story
Before Your throne, our crowns we'll bring
And praises to our God we'll sing

Worthy, worthy are You God
To receive all glory, laud
For You created everything
Even the rewards we bring

Unto You, Lord, belongs all glory
Our treasure and riches will tell the story
Of a lifetime spent in love and giving
There still is time while you are among the living....

March 8, 2014

Matthew 6:1-4
Revelation 4:9-11
1 Corinthians 3:12-15

One morning I was reflecting on something the Lord had taught me many years ago. As I was reviewing it in my mind this poem came to me.

A long time ago, I had been involved in the leadership of a ministry for a number of years. It was very successful and many other people had also been involved in its operation. As they reached the end of their term, which was usually short, the leader of the group would thank them at the monthly meeting and present them with a small gift. He would list all the things they did and commend them for their faithful service.

When I felt led to leave the ministry after being there a number of years, really almost from the start of the group, this leader barely acknowledged I would no longer be with them. It was just a short mention that someone else would be taking my place. There was no mention of all the positions I had held or my faithfulness for all the years in leadership.

The next day I was letting it bother me that I was not recognized for all I had done.

Then I heard a still small voice in my mind that was not audible to the ear. "Who did you do all that for"?

"Well of course for You", I replied to the Lord.

"Well then, why are you looking for praise from man"? The still small voice continued, "If you wish I would change the circumstances and allow you to have the praise of man, but then you would forfeit the reward I have for you which is very great and eternal."

I instantly felt very foolish and humbled. The choice was before me to have the praise of man or the delayed praise of God. "Forgive me Lord, I replied, for looking here for my reward. I would much prefer my treasure to be stored in heaven awaiting me there". And I meant it with all my heart. It changed me forever.

Now, when I do something for the Lord, I find myself thanking Him for not being recognized. It is like a private joke between us. I tell Him, "Thank you Lord, for hiding what I did. I would rather have Your thanks and reward".

My Very Great Reward

Do not neglect so great a salvation
For the pleasures of this life can lead to devastation
The temptations, they glitter, to the lust of the eye
Its promise, when fulfilled, is just a big lie

Help to keep my feet, Lord, on the path of life
For the way is narrow and filled with strife
Give me Your hand to guide and direct
As You send Your angels to help and protect

At the end of this path awaits heaven's door
It opens to wonders and life evermore
"For I am Your shield and Your very great reward
Find your delight in Me", says the Lord

February 27, 2016

Genesis 15:1 – "After this, the word of the Lord came to Abram in a vision: "Do not be afraid, Abram. I am your shield, your very great reward."

Hebrews 2:1-4
James 4:1-3
John 14:6
Matthew 7:13-14
Hebrews 11:8-16
Psalm 84:4-7
Psalm 37:4

If You Knew the Reward

If you knew the reward, it would bring you great joy
When you do things for Me that you do not enjoy
Every cup that you fill, every tear that you dry
Will result in great riches as eternity rolls by

I looked down from heaven to seek after the lost
The way was not easy and came at great cost
I gave up My Son so the way could be laid
To purchase their pardon a ransom was paid

It is not too late to store up great treasure
That is held in your name and will bring you much pleasure
For the days grow short and My return is nigh
Sow while it is day, the night will quickly come by

March 13, 2017

Matthew 25:31-46
Matthew 6:1-4, 19-24
Matthew 13:1-23, 44-52

Life's Reward

One day the cares of life will be over
Eternity will loom before us forever
Our place will be set in God's kingdom on high
Did we work hard for Him, or only enough to get by?

A fire will test all the offerings we bring
As the angels are watching on hovering wing
Will ashes remain or treasures so bright?
The "Day" will reveal and bring it to light

Each will be rewarded according to their labor
Was our love only for us, or did it extend to our neighbor?
Our motives and work will be shown for what it is
Was it for our own glory or was it for His?

For those who suffered and for His Name fought
To those overcomers crowns will be brought
For those who were faithful and His promises did claim
On those overcomers will He write His new name

The choice before us is to surrender to Him
Or live for ourselves with faith and love growing dim
Come Holy Spirit refine my gold in the fire
As I seek to please my Savior with wholehearted desire

September 13, 2016

1 Corinthians 3:1-15
Revelation 2:8-11
Revelation 3:7-13
Revelation 3:14-18

Our Search for Significance

God tests a person by being praised
Will his heart remain humble or will it be raised?
Even though the Lord knows the way we will take
The drama plays out for heaven's own sake

We need to know what is in our own heart
To ask for wisdom is the place we must start
Flattering words test our hidden desires
Bringing them to light by the Spirits bright fire

We search for significance all the day long
To want our lives to matter is never wrong
But, for whose glory do we really seek?
Our actions declare if we are proud or are meek

Come learn from Me for I am lowly and humble
If you take up My yoke you will never with pride stumble
The eye of the Lord goes throughout the whole earth
Jesus died on the cross to proclaim our true worth

Death could not hold Him – He arose from the grave
If you believe He died for you – then you are saved
Everything you do and all that you say
Is recorded in books, to be revealed on that "Day"

Then you will understand – it will be revealed with fire
The "Day" will declare all your hidden desires
Your search will be over – will treasure remain?
Or will you suffer loss with only heaven to gain?

August 15, 2016

Proverbs 27:21 (NLT) – "Fire tests the purity of silver and gold, but a person is tested by being praised."

Acts 12:21-23
Matthew 11:28-30
Ephesians 4:29-30
Romans 8:18-25
Philippians 3:17-21
1 Corinthians 3:10-15

The Bride Brought Forth

My bride will be clothed in rich gold of Ophir
For she is worthy of all the gifts I do give her
My beloved was faithful through the journey called life
In eternity past she was called as My wife

This life is a test that will be proved true by fires
These flames will reveal secret thoughts and desires
This refined gold will be woven with care
Into beautiful garments My redeemed saints will wear

Costly stones and silver will adorn My beloved
As she is brought to the King to be joyfully wedded
There never again will be such sights and sounds
At a marriage feast where God's love joyfully abounds

Eternity will reveal all the choices made on earth
Of treasure stored in heaven proved to be of great worth
But riches hoarded here will one day be gone
So be careful what you build your life and dreams upon

December 9, 2016

Psalm 45:9, 13, 14
1 Corinthians 3:12-15
Revelation 19:6-8
Isaiah 61:3
Revelation 3:18

Psalm 45 is a song in praise of a conquering king on his wedding day, probably someone belonging to David's dynasty. Many believe this king is a type or foreshadowing of Christ. It may also be called a hidden prophetic picture of Christ and His future bride. This Psalm corresponds to the story in Revelation 19 and the book of the Song of Solomon.

While studying Psalm 45 one morning I meditated on verses 9, 13 and 14. These words tell of the bride being brought forth to the King and describe what she is wearing. Her embroidered garments were interwoven with gold. That would take some time to make. To be beautiful to her, it would take into account her personal preferences and taste, so these garments were made ahead of time according to her directions.

Then I thought of Revelation 19:6-8 which describes the wedding of the Lamb. The clothes given to the bride stood for the righteous acts of the saints. So she was clothed symbolically with all the good things she had done on earth.

Verses in 1 Corinthians 3:10-15 then came to mind. Our works done in this life will be tested with fire one "Day". The things done for the Lord will shine forth as gold, silver, and precious stones which will survive through eternity. Other selfish things we have done will perish in that fire and be of no future use to us. The apathetic Laodicean church was counseled in Revelation 3:18 to buy gold refined in the fire from the Lord and white clothes to cover their shameful nakedness. To those who overcame this apathy He promised they would have the right to sit on the throne with Him.

Is it possible, I wondered, that some of this gold, silver, and jewels that survive this fire might be embroidered in the very fabric of the white robes we will be given as the bride of Christ? My mind staggered at the thought that possibly our future wedding garments might personally be embroidered now out of the trials and triumphs of this life.

As I sat undone by the beauty of this symbolic meaning of the garments of the bride, I asked the Lord for a poem to help me understand all these verses. The poem above is an answer to that prayer.

Prayer: Lord, how can I even imagine the future honor You have revealed to us as the bride of Christ. Help us to live lives worthy of all You have called us to do. We ask for the Holy Spirits help to make us pure and spotless in mind and deed as we get ready for that day. Even in times of despair in this life we choose to put on a garment of praise, for this will result in the display of Your splendor. We want to honor You by our lives, for You are our Lord.

He Who Overcomes

I can overcome by the blood of the Lamb
For the One who stands with me is the great "I AM"
Hear what the Spirit says to the bride
"Nothing can harm you if in Jesus you abide"

He who overcomes will I give the right to eat
From the Tree of Life bearing abundant fruit so sweet
Be faithful even to death and I will give you life
For the suffering you endured, I will crown you as My wife

To him who overcomes and does My will to the end
Will receive authority over nations and go where I send
For you did not love your life so much as to shrink from death
Your life was your testimony even til final breath

He who overcomes will be dressed in white
In the Book of Life his name will I write
I will never blot out his name because he was faithful to Me
But will acknowledge his name before heavenly company

Therefore, rejoice, all of heaven and earth
A new day is dawning and will soon give birth
Salvation, glory and power belong to our God
He will reign with justice and an iron scepter rod

April 20, 2017

Psalm 121
Revelation 12:11-12
Revelation 2:7-11
Revelation 2:26-27
Revelation 3:4-5

Chapter 9

The Harvest

The Harvest

From His side poured out blood and water
Redemption has come to earth's sons and daughters
Hanging on the cross Jesus bled and died
The Savior took our place on Calvary's side

When the harvest is ripe He'll return on a cloud
The time of reaping will come for the unrepentant and proud
With a crown on His head and a sickle in His hand
The swinging will start throughout all the lands

The clusters of grapes will be sheared from earth's vine
And squeezed into the cup of God's wrath as fine wine
With His garments stained red from the trampling of nations
He will make them to drink in great tribulation

For the Lord has a sacrifice in Bozrah to show
On the day of His wrath a blood river will flow
They will be trampled in the winepress outside the city
He will not relent or show any pity

The one who will do this is the Lord, alone
The nations will reap what on earth they had sown
For the harvest is ripe, both the bad and the good
Gather the wheat into the barn but leave the rest as firewood

January 2, 2016

Revelation 14:14-20
Isaiah 63:1-6, Isaiah 34:1-8
Psalm 110:5-7
Joel 3:1-3
Joel 3:12-14
Isaiah 14:24-27
Matthew 13:24-30 & 36-43
Jeremiah 25:27-33

Matthew 3:11-12 – "I baptize you with water for repentance. But after me comes one who is more powerful than I, whose sandals I am not worthy to carry. He will baptize you with the Holy Spirit and fire. ¹² His winnowing fork is in his hand, and he will clear his threshing floor, gathering his wheat into the barn and burning up the chaff with unquenchable fire."

Matthew 13:39 – "....The harvest is the end of the age, and the harvesters are angels."

These scripture verses on this subject are hard to read, yes, even harder to believe they will one day happen.

To those who think they will only be fulfilled figuratively, which verses were fulfilled that way at Christ's first coming? Did not all those literally happen just as the Bible predicted?

The angels will help to gather the harvest but the Word makes it clear the Lord alone will do the trampling.

For those who accept that Jesus, the Son of God, came to die and take our place so we don't have to suffer the wrath of God, for those, this judgment won't happen to them. Their names are written in the Book of Life. This salvation is offered to anyone no matter how many sins were committed. Anyone's path in life can be changed.

Prayer: Lord, I pray that anyone reading this who doesn't know You will ask You to be their Savior and Lord so they will not have to go through this wrath. Come into their heart and change them into Your image so the world might see the difference between those who believe and those who do not.

Special Reflection:

The day before I wrote this, I saw a story on the internet about a worker who was repairing an elevator on a cruise ship and was crushed above the doors. Witnesses said the blood poured down the elevator door like a fountain and sounded like it was raining. They had pictures of the door and I couldn't believe so much blood came from one body.

It got me thinking about the day of the Lord and the scriptures that prophesy of the day Christ will trample His enemies. When men die in battle a river of blood doesn't form. It is when they are crushed or trampled that this would happen. In Revelation the river of blood is said to be about 180 miles long. That is something I can't even imagine.

The Latter Rain

The lightning flashes, the thunder roars
Illuminating the steeple and the churches' front doors
The time has come for the deluge to begin
It is the latter rain of the Spirit's outpouring

The storm clouds are gathering, the wind starts to blow
As workers struggle to bring in the harvest below
The Lord's hand delays, bringing a small reprieve
So the crop can be brought to repentance and believe

The fire from hell's pit is dancing up high
As screams from those trapped there reaches night's sky
It is too late for those who rejected God's plea
To depart from their sin and plead for mercy

The flood of God's Spirit pours out visions and dreams
On the young and the old in glory filled streams
In their new found strength the workers rejoice
As hope infuses their bodies and voice

The glory of God starts to cover the earth
And pushes back darkness, declaring God's worth
Nations will come to the brightness of God's light
As His Word is believed, and the blind receive sight

This time of great harvest will soon come to an end
God's Spirit with man will not always contend
But now the time has come for the deluge to begin
It is the latter rain of the Spirit's outpouring

February 16, 2017

John 4:10-13
John 7:37-39
Deuteronomy 11:13-15 KJV
Isaiah 44:1-5
Joel 2:28-29

Isaiah 60:1-3
Genesis 6:3
Isaiah 66:22-24

As I sat praying this morning, I asked the Lord what was on His heart. As I quietly listened a picture came in my mind of a flash of lightning illuminating the steeple of a church. As I wrote this down the rest of the poem quickly followed.

Water is a symbol of the Holy Spirit. Rain, therefore, can symbolize the outpouring of the Holy Spirit or revival.

There are autumn and spring rains in the Middle East. The rainy season in Israel begins in October and ends in April. The autumn rains gently water the ground to prepare it for the seed. The spring rains called the latter rains are much heavier and plump the ears of grain after the plant matures. In between the former and latter rains there is a dry period in which knots are formed along the stalk as it becomes dry and hardens. This is necessary so the green stalks don't fall over and lay on the ground.

We see a picture of this harvest cycle in the Spirit's outpouring at Pentecost. Seeds were planted all across the known world and the rain of the Spirit watered the seed. Then came a dry period, dark ages, where God's power and glory seemed to not be as manifest as in earlier times. In the last century we started to see the return of the rains again, revivals springing up everywhere. This is the start of the last outpouring of the Holy Spirit. The latter rains are always heavier and come right before the harvest.

John 4:35-36 – "³⁵ Don't you have a saying, 'It's still four months until harvest'? I tell you, open your eyes and look at the fields! They are ripe for harvest. ³⁶ Even now the one who reaps draws a wage and harvests a crop for eternal life, so that the sower and the reaper may be glad together."

The Bride Awakened

Let the bride be revealed in all of her glory
Eternity will witness the telling of her story
For in the time of great darkness that came upon earth
The Lord's light rose upon her revealing her worth

This caused the nations to be drawn to that light
Removing the veils that covered man's sight
Even kings were drawn to the brightness of her dawn
As the morning star rose in her heart with a song

So sweet a melody came forth, it hushed the birds sound
Causing grace and mercy o'er the earth to abound
The riches of the nations will be brought to the Lord
As He opens His hands and His Spirit's outpoured

Then you will know that I, the Lord, am your Savior
When I visit the earth with My love and My favor
Even creation groans and awaits My return
For My redemption to come do they eagerly yearn

You will call your walls Salvation and your gates Praise
As you dwell in My presence and on My face gaze
I will be your everlasting light and your glory
For you will be My witness telling redemptions story

145

Debbie Furey

February 25, 2016

Revelation 19:7-8
Isaiah 60
2 Peter 1:19
Romans 8:18-23

    The excerpt below is adapted from the book, "The Days of His Presence", by Pastor Frangipane:

The Morning Star

The day of the Lord, like the dawning of any calendar day, does not burst forth abruptly. It is not pitch black at 5:59 a.m. and then, suddenly, bright morning the next minute. The night sky gradually recedes, retreating from the approaching rays of light. Even before the dawn breaks, the morning star faithfully heralds the coming day, announcing to the world still in darkness that light is at hand.

Some may ask, doesn't the Bible warn that the day of the Lord would come as a "thief in the night"? Yes, but His coming as a thief is only to the backslidden and sinner. Paul says, "But you, brethren, are not in darkness, that the day would overtake you like a thief; for you are all sons of light and sons of day. We are not of night nor of darkness" (1 Thess 5:4-5).

Indeed, the Scriptures use the image of the morning star to depict the church at the end of the age. This visual portrays well the reality that awaits us.

Concerning the end times, Peter wrote:

"So we have the prophetic word made more sure, to which you do well to pay attention as to a lamp shining in a dark place, until the day dawns and the morning star arises in your hearts" (2 Pet. 1:19).

The ancients were fully aware that the morning star appeared while it was still night. The morning star, which is actually the planet Venus, is situated in our sky just above the eastern horizon. It is perfectly positioned to reflect the light of the coming day before the sunrise. The light of the morning star is a small, but beautiful, preview of the coming day. Here, Peter is saying that before the day of the Lord breaks, the morning star shall rise in our hearts!

We generate no light ourselves. It is only our position at the end of the age that enables us to reflect the day that is coming -- all the glory belongs to Jesus! He is Himself the "bright morning star" (Rev. 22:16). This unveiling of Christ rising in His people, like the morning star before dawn, is perfectly consistent with Isaiah's word: "Arise, shine; for your light has come, and the glory of the Lord has risen upon you" (Isa. 60:1).

When will the glory rise? Just as the morning star rises while it is still night, so the glory of God shall rise within us when "darkness will cover the earth and deep darkness the peoples" (v. 2).

Are you ready for the manifestation of the Lord's glory? Are you preparing to be indwelt by the fullness of Christ?

Reprinted with permission from Francis Frangipane – www.frangipane.org and www.arrowbookstore.com

Sensing Your Ways

Take away my heart of stone
And fix my thoughts on You alone
Open up my eyes to see
The wounded hearts of humanity

Cause my ears to hear the sound
You're sending forth to release those bound
Give my mouth the words to speak
To ones who are discouraged, weak

Guide my hands to touch those lost
And let them know You paid the cost
You carried their sins to Calvary's hill
The requirements of the law to fulfill

Oh taste and see that the Lord is good
You'd fear the Lord if you understood
That the ways of the world lead to death
Know the enemy comes to steal your breath

The fragrance of the Lord is sweet
For those who go in prayer to meet
The presence of the Lord comes down
Where two or more are gathered round

Help me sense Your ways Oh Lord
Ground my faith daily in Your Word
Till at last we in heaven will meet
And Your enemies are gathered under Your feet

October 15, 2016

Ezekiel 11:18-21
Matthew 25: 31:36
Psalm 34
Matthew 18:19-20
John 14:6
1 Corinthians 15:24-28

Gather My Harvest

Lord, help me not waste a single day
As the world grows darker and from Thy truth they stray
For the time grows short when our light can be seen
The dark forces make plans that can't be foreseen

Wake up, O sleeper, and rise from your rest
For the fields are ripe and ready for harvest
The storms are approaching, proclaim and warn
So the crop can be brought safely into My barn

Even the demons will submit in My name
Releasing their captives, the blind and the lame
You will overcome by the blood of the Lamb
The One who goes with you is the great "I AM"

Gather My harvest so My house can be full
I am coming soon, to reign and to rule
My bride will be on the throne by My side
A new world is coming where we will all abide

June 17, 2016

Ephesians 5:8-21
John 4:35-38
Matthew 9:35-38
Luke 10:1-20
Revelation 12:10-12
Revelation 21

Storm Clouds Gathering

I see the tears of the oppressed
Of those downtrodden and distressed
They have no comforter that sees
They have no hope, no life, and no peace

Where are those that I can send?
Who can help, heal, and defend?
Arise and light your darkened lamp
Call fire from heaven to empower, encamp

I send My wind to fan your soul
Ask for oil to fill your lamps' bowl
Open the door and come join Me
The harvest field lies ripe and ready

A storm is coming there is not much time
For the enemy is working overtime
His storm clouds threaten to destroy
My waiting crop that is My joy

Come join Me now, it's not too late
To lead the lost to heaven's gate
I'll dry their tears and heal their heart
My grace and mercy I'll joyfully impart

December 26, 2016

Ecclesiastes 4:1
Isaiah 6:8
Isaiah 60:1-3
Song of Solomon 5:2
Revelation 3:19-20
John 4:34-38

As I was praying in the last week of the year, I asked the Lord, "What is important to You"? I wanted to know what was on the Lord's heart for the coming New Year. As I waited, I asked for a poem from Him. This is what I got.

Chapter 10
Be Ready

Debbie Furey

Be Ready

Lo! I hear the turtledove cooing
It is the voice of my Bridegroom tenderly wooing
Saying "Come away my love
To a place that I've prepared above"

The Lord is coming for a spotless bride
For those left behind, there will be no place to hide
They will look; they will grieve, and sit to ponder
But the door will be closed in the sky up yonder

Be ready, be ready, My lovely bride
Prepare yourself to reign by My side
For a new world is coming and there will be peace
I will reign with My enemies under My feet.

2011

Song of Solomon 2
Matthew 25:1-13
Psalm 110

Do you hear the sound of the Spirit calling? It is ever so faint, yet so alluring. The business of day easily drowns it out. You must set time aside and sit in the presence of the Lord to hear it. Sometimes if you are awakened at night, listen closely. Thoughts will fill your mind that didn't originate from your understanding. Pursue those fleeting images and ask the Lord what they mean. He might be trying to tell you something. That is how I get a lot of these poems. When your heart is still and it is quiet around you, listen....

Prayer: Help me to be more organized at home, Lord, so that I might find more time to be in Your presence and reading Your word. I need to reject doing those frivolous things that captivate me to make time for things that have lasting value. Open my ears to hear Your Spirit gently calling me aside. Give me Your wisdom as I read Your word. Fill my heart with Your love so that I have it to give away freely during the day.

The Beauty of the Bride

Sweet music plays as the bride does sleep
The strains do lull as the slumber grows deep
The Lord's heart quickens as He tries to shake
For the day is approaching for her to awake

The beauty of the bride is something to behold
It is the making of a legend to be forever told
Throughout the whole land there is no one more fair
From her dainty small feet to her long flowing hair

Debbie Furey

Her eyes are like pools of water that are deep
While full soft lips breathe music so sweet
The beloved's skin glows, there is no flaw
Her form is shapely and her hands are small

She moves with a grace and gentleness so rare
Throughout the whole land there is none that compare
The bride's robe is spotless so pure and white
While her quiet spirit exudes strength and might

The Lord's heart quickens, again He will shake
She hears His voice and tries to awake
"I must get ready, He will be here soon"
So she lights her lamp by the glow of the moon

The bride knew He would come in the black of night
So she gathered her oil to make her lamp bright
The beloved one prepared thinking only of Him
While the foolish ones played and their eyes grew dim

The door was opened and the bride stepped in
She was ready and waiting for her new life to begin
The banquet was ready and the groom was there
As the saints were gathered together in the air

The door was then shut to those only hoping
Even though they begged for the door to be opened
Therefore, keep watch, for you don't know the hour
That the Lord will come in His majesty and power

He is coming for a bride that is spotless and pure
For those who overcome the evil day and endure
Together, forever, we will be by His side
Get ready, get ready says the wise bride

September 14, 2015

Revelation 22:17 – "The Spirit and the bride say, "Come!" And let the one who hears say, "Come!" Let the one who is thirsty come; and let the one who wishes take the free gift of the water of life."

1 Peter 3:1-6
Isaiah 61:10
Song of Solomon 4:1-15
Song of Solomon 7:1-9
Matthew 25:1-13
1 Thessalonians 4:17
Revelation 2
Revelation3
Romans 13:11-14

Awaking early one morning, the song, "Give Me Jesus", played softly and peacefully in my heart. It had been one of the songs the worship team had played on Sunday. Then, I asked the Lord what was on His heart.

I got the title to this poem first and started writing it. Then I pictured in my mind the hands of a conductor tapping his music stand with a baton and starting to wave the stick softly. The first line appeared in my mind. In the next few hours, the poem slowly materialized.

Oh, bride of the Lord, do you see how beautiful you are to Him? He wants you to know that. He wants you to know how much He loves you. That is what is on His heart, thoughts of you.

Prayer: Help me to wake up from my deep sleep Lord and prepare to meet You. Fill me with the oil from Your Holy Spirit for "Your word is a light unto my feet and a light unto my path". In this time of great darkness on the earth, I pray Your light in me will shine to the darkest corners of the earth for Your glory. May Your wise bride bring in a great harvest of souls for Your kingdom in these coming dark days.

I heard a saying once – "To walk in the truth of the gospel will cost us everything now; To not walk in it will cost us everything later."

Remove the Dross

Get ready, get ready, My love, My desire
The refinement procedure does include fire
For in this process the dross will arise
Impurities will surface that have been hindering the wise

Get ready; get ready to remove this dross
Failure to do so will reveal a tremendous cost
For if it remains and the mixture gets coolish
The result is a bride that acts very foolish

How will you know when no dross is detected?
You will look in the mirror and see Me reflected
Christ in you, the hope of your glory
To be joined with Me is your song and your story

Get ready, get ready, and make your robe white
Put holy salve on your eyes to give you new sight
I am behind the lattice waiting at the door
Will you hear Me knocking or My voice implore?

Ten virgins were waiting, but only five could go in
For five were foolish and harbored sin
But five were wise and hurriedly prepared
To meet with their Bridegroom up in the air

Get ready, get ready come dine with Me
Our love will last throughout eternity
Those that overcome will I give the right
To sit on My throne forever in My sight

September 17, 2014

Malachi 3:1-4
Colossians 1:27-29
Colossians 3:1-17
Revelation 3:14-22
Song of Solomon 2:8-10
Matthew 25:1-13
1 Thessalonians 4:13-18
1 Peter 4:12-17
Romans 13:11-14

To understand this poem, you have to understand how the refinement of gold and silver happens. The refiner sits at the melted pot of gold or silver and heats the metal to a liquid stage. Impurities, called dross, then come to the surface where they can be skimmed off. If they are not skimmed off, when the metal cools down, the impurities then mingle back in with the metal. To further remove the remaining impurities the refiner needs to turn the heat back up again to bring them to the surface.

When a refining fire happens in our lives, and brings sin to the surface to deal with, we need to get rid of the impurities in our life hindering our relationship with God. If not, don't be surprised to find the heat getting turned up again and again. The Lord does this to discipline and purify us, not destroy us.

How do we know when the dross is gone from the pot of gold? When the refiner looks in the pot and sees his reflection staring back at him.

Malachi tells of the Lord coming back suddenly, and being like a refiner's fire and a cleansing soap.

We need to be overcomers, for the reward is very great.

Malachi 3:1-4 - "I will send my messenger, who will prepare the way before me. Then suddenly the Lord you are seeking will come to his temple; the messenger of the covenant, whom you desire, will come," says the Lord Almighty.
² But who can endure the day of his coming? Who can stand when he appears? For he will be like a refiner's fire or a launderer's soap. ³ He will sit as a refiner and purifier of silver; he will purify the Levites and refine them like gold and silver. Then the Lord will have men who will bring offerings in righteousness, ⁴ and the offerings of Judah and Jerusalem will be acceptable to the Lord, as in days gone by, as in former years."

A Message to the Laodicean Church

Lord, give me the truth, I will not despise
A healing salve to put in my eyes
Eyes that are weakened by sin and blame
Can be cured by the Master for those suffering shame

He is coming for a bride who is spotless and pure
For the one who is ready, the one who endures
Wake up O wise one from your deep sleep
Relight the flame in the lamp you do keep

Get ready, get ready, My beloved, My joy
Dust off your Bible and My Word employ
For I am coming for those whose hearts are aflame
Your deeds will reveal your hearts true claim

You say "I am rich and don't need a thing"
But you are wretched, blind, poor and despairing
Come, buy from Me gold refined in the fire
So you can be rich, clothed, healed and desired

Those whom I love, I rebuke and chasten
Come, repent quickly so My return can hasten
I am outside, knocking, please open the door
For fellowship sweet My voice does implore

Those who hear and let Me come in
Will be overcomers of the flesh and of sin
Drawing strength from My presence as you sit by My side
My glory rests upon you when in Me you abide

To him who overcomes will I give the right
To sit with Me on My throne in the Father's sight
For those who are ashamed of Me on the earth
Will not partake of Me and the second birth

January 2, 2015

Revelation 3:14-22
Matthew 25:1-13
Mark 8:34-38
Romans 1:16-17

Double Minded

Ask from Me wisdom to stay on life's path
For broad is the road that leads to destruction and wrath
You cannot get to heaven by just calling Me Lord
If you love Me, you will keep My Word

I open My arms and call each by name
My blood can wash clean all your guilt and your shame
But you must choose Me and leave sin behind
To live on both paths reveals a double mind

Draw near to Me and I will draw near to you
Purify your hearts with Morning Star's dew
Humble yourselves and I will lift you up
Open the door and together we'll sup

Only those who overcome can sit on My throne
Just as I overcame and have become the cornerstone
Fix your eyes on Me and with perseverance run the race
I run alongside of you supplying mercy and grace

April 19, 2017

Matthew 7:13-27
James 1:2-8
James 4:4-10
Revelation 22:16
Isaiah 26:19
Hosea 14:4-9
Revelation 3:19-22
Hebrews 12:1-13

Morning Star's dew is a word picture of God's favor, instruction and freedom. The Morning Star is Jesus – Revelation 22:16. The morning star is a bright light seen in the heavens just before morning breaks.

In Song of Solomon 5:2-7, there is a prophetic picture of the Beloved coming to His bride, the Church, in the night with His head drenched with

Debbie Furey

dew. He is coming to invite her to join Him but she is not ready so He withdraws. In these verses we see *favor* is removed from her.

Zechariah prophesied in Luke 1:78-79 about a rising sun (Son) coming from heaven to guide our feet into the path of peace – *instruction*.

Malachi 4:2-3 also mentions this sun (Son) of righteousness arising with healing in its wings. This rising will cause us to be released from our stalls like calves – *freedom*. Then the wicked will be trampled under our feet.

How do we purify our hearts with Morning Star's dew? We humble ourselves and draw near to God. This releases God's favor, instruction and freedom.

The opposite is pride. God opposes the proud but gives grace (favor) to the humble. 1 Peter 5:5.

Prayer: Forgive me Lord for all the times I live with a double mind. Purify my thoughts and desires and give me singleness of heart to love and worship You in holiness.

Mount Up With Eagles Wings

Mount up with eagles wings to take higher ground
You are seated with Christ and not just earth-bound
Soaring on thermals that can't be seen with the eye
Increases our vision as we circle and fly

The Holy Spirit is the wind under our wings
He carries us higher as we joyfully sing
Though we can't see Him we know He is there
He ushers us to God's presence high up in the air

By attaining higher ground, we will receive grace
To overcome the enemy we every day face
Defend your territory that God has given you
Till night has ended and you see morning's dew

Make your nest high up in the trees
The Lord, your defender, is the "One who sees"
Raise up the young ones with diligence and care
The enemy will come to steal, so beware

Seek the Lord while He may be found
Respond to Him – He is calling you to higher ground
He is teaching us to rule and reign with Him
Don't miss your chance by choosing earthly whims

April 10, 2017

Isaiah 40:28-31
Ephesians 2:1-10
Psalm 30:1-5
Genesis 16:13-14
2 Timothy 2:1-13

Get on the Bus

Get on the bus, it's not too late
The mission has started and already left the gate
If you are not ready, it will leave without you
It is the adventure of a lifetime says the "Faithful and True"

Worldly pleasures have lulled the saints to sleep
But a cry is going forth to those in slumber deep
"The Bridegroom is coming, go forth to meet Him
Prepare your lamp for day's light grows dim"

Gross darkness is coming to cover the lost
It will shroud the earth like a bush covered in frost
Hearts will grow cold and eyes will not see
Lovers of pleasure instead of God they will be

A light will arise like the spreading of dawn
To this great brilliance will many be drawn
It is the glory of the Lord that will shine upon you
Pushing back darkness releasing Morning Star's dew

Come, all who are thirsty, it's not too late
God's mission has started, do not hesitate
If you are not ready, it will leave without you
It's the adventure of a lifetime says the "Faithful and True"

March 27, 2017

Matthew 25:1-13
Isaiah 60:1-3
Romans 1:21
2 Timothy 3:1-9
Isaiah 55

Revelation 19:

"[11] I saw heaven standing open and there before me was a white horse, whose rider is called Faithful and True. With justice he judges and wages war."
"[14] The armies of heaven were following him, riding on white horses and dressed in fine linen, white and clean."
"[19] Then I saw the beast and the kings of the earth and their armies gathered together to wage war against the rider on the horse and his army."

I awoke this morning with a dream already fading in my mind. I was on a tour and the schedule was changed. Most of the people were already on the bus because they were prepared and ready. It departed and went somewhere but then met up with someone who was not ready when it had left the first time. They were able then to get on and join the group. As I was thinking about this dream, this poem came to me.

Prayer: Help me to wake up from my slumber, Lord, and prepare to go with You, wherever You may lead. Forgive me for preferring to sleep in and be distracted by the things of the world. I don't want to miss the bus. Fill me with Your Holy Spirit and let Your glory reflect off me to a world filled with darkness. I want to follow You wherever You may lead.

Debbie Furey

The Fear of the Lord

The fear of the Lord will keep you from falling
So heed its voice when you hear it calling
"Don't do that, turn and run-away"
Is one of the things you will hear it say

The fear of the Lord is a fountain of life
All who see its beauty will cease from strife
Its splashing water cleanses our heart
If we listen closely, from sin we'll depart

Don't believe the lie, "you can't fall from grace"
For only the pure in heart will see God's face
Be afraid; be afraid to turn from "the Way"
For the pleasures of life can lead us astray

The fear of the Lord is the beginning of wisdom
By the Blood of the Lamb we overcome
Wisdom calls out to those going by
"Whoever finds me will live and not die"

The fear of the Lord endures forever
From His love we can never be severed
Lord, who may dwell on Your holy hill?
"Those who are blameless and love Me, will"

February 26, 2017

Proverbs 14:27
John 15:5-6
Hebrews 6:4-12
Hebrews 10:26-39
2 Peter 2:17-22
2 Peter 3:17-18
Romans 11:17-22
Ezekiel 18:19-32
2 Timothy 2:12
Proverbs 8, and 9
Psalms 19:9
Psalm 15

Our New President

A new day is dawning across our land
Warring angels are being dispatched to take a mighty stand
I have heard your prayers and am mighty to save
The land of the free, and the home of the brave

Let your faith and hope be mixed equally with love
As I direct My earthly army with strategies from above
When you hear the sound of marching, fall on your knees
It is the heavenly passing ahead of you creating an opening breeze

Debbie Furey

Cease not your prayers for the man I did select
For the enemies plan includes mockery and disrespect
Work with one hand and in the other hold a sword
For My Word will go out mightily as the Spirit is outpoured

My fire will surround you; I will be your glory within
As you depart from evil and abandon your sin
I will answer your prayers as you humbly look to Me
As your nation is restored to freedom and liberty

January 20, 2017

1 Chronicles 14:13-17
Nehemiah 2:11-20
Nehemiah 4
Zechariah 2:3-5

As I prayed for my country and the new president on the morning of the Presidential Inauguration, this poem came to me.

Chapter 11
The Day of the Lord

The Day of the Lord

An overwhelming scourge will pass through the land
A day of darkness, the day of the Lord is at hand
Hills will be leveled and the valleys raised up
The birds of prey will be invited to sup

Nations will gather against My anointed
The seed of the serpent will be self-appointed
This idol shepherd will scatter the sheep
Demons will be released from the caverns of the deep

Woe to those who live on the earth
For they have rejected Me and the second birth
I have given them over, it will be their hour
The cities of the earth will be in the serpent's power

Those days will be cut short and the Lord will arise
He'll come in the clouds, His glory filling the skies
The lightening will flash and the earth will roar
As the King of Kings on His white steed will soar

The wicked will be slain by the sword in His mouth
As He heads down to Bozrah which is further south
He will set up His kingdom which will be without end
To the lake of fire, His enemies He will send.

He will reign with justice and a rod of iron
Comforting His people as He rules in Zion
The Ancient of Days will take His seat
Feeding His children with the finest of wheat

April 13, 2015

Joel 2	Daniel 7:21-27
Genesis 3:15	Isaiah 34:1-8
Zechariah 11:16-17 KJV	Isaiah 63:1-6
Revelation 9:1-11	Daniel 11:31-45
John 3:1-21	Daniel 12
Revelation 16:17-20	

Dark Forces Rising

The watchers are watching, come and take heed
Destruction and death are the plans they do seed
Dark forces are rising to cover the earth
Dark forces are rising and giving birth

A grey mist appears and takes a new form
Demonic forces on the wings of a storm
They think they are hidden, they think no one sees
But mighty is God of the earth, wind, and seas

Like tares they are planted amongst the good grain
Counterfeiting the holy, are the profane
Until the harvest leave them to grow
To pluck them out now, will bring others woe

Come gather the harvest into God's barn
The storm is approaching, proclaim and warn
Dark forces are rising to cover the earth
Dark forces are rising and giving birth

Our Lord is mighty over wind, sea and land
On the threshing floor, His winnowing fork is in hand
On the wind of the Spirit, His wheat will be sifted
Into the fire the tares will be lifted

Who will you follow, who gave you birth?
Are you seated above, or is your home the earth?
Make a choice, the time is growing short
Dark forces are rising and coming forth

May 21, 2014

Matthew 3:12
Matthew 13:24-30
Malachi 4

We do not need to fear. I don't remember who said this, but I wrote it in my bible, "Safety is not the absence of danger, but the presence of God". What an awesome thought! For, there is no place on earth that can be truly safe. This is a fallen world with unseen dangers always around us. If your heart is fearful, read the Psalms. Most of the ones King David wrote will fill you with faith in the "God who sees".

Prayer: In our natural strength, Lord, we are so weak compared to the supernatural demonic forces. But, because You are with us and for us, we do not have to fear. Indeed, You are even allowing the enemies plans that come against Your people to train us to do battle and teach us how to be victorious. How can we learn to reign if everything always goes our way? Keep me close to You. Guide me in the way I should go. Train my fingers for battle and my hands for war.

A Day of Darkness

The chariot wheels are turning, turning
The fortifications are burning, burning
Mayhem everywhere shouts and screaming
Generals plotting and evil scheming

The day of the Lord has finally come
Men's hopes and dreams have come undone
It is a day of darkness and not of light
It is a day when justice has no sight

The earth will shake and the waters roar
Birds of prey will gorge and soar
Men's hearts will fail and fear will win
They will continue to love their sin

The Lord will mourn over each one lost
They will not repent and count the cost
So bowls of wrath will be poured out
Causing the earth to reel about

In the midst of this darkness a light will arise
He will be called Wonderful, Counselor, Son of the Most High
His reign on the earth will be without end
To the lake of fire His enemies He sends

God's glory and grace will fill the whole earth
His subjects are those who choose the new birth
This new creation will surpass the old
Mysteries revealed, wonders to behold

October 23, 2015

Revelation 9:20-21
Revelation 16
Isaiah 9:1-7
Malachi 4:2
Isaiah 65:17-25
Revelation 21

Isaiah 66:15,18 – "See, the LORD is coming with fire, and his chariots are like a whirlwind; he will bring down his anger with fury, and his rebuke with flames of fire."
"And I, because of what they have planned and done, am about to come and gather the people of all nations and languages, and they will come and see my glory."

When Truth Has Stumbled

When truth has stumbled in the streets
And those who dine on sin do eat
The way of peace they do not know
Their paths are crooked, dark and low

Then justice stands afar from us
And weeps with cries so piteous
Like the blind we grope along the wall
The strong, the weak, we stumble, fall

Then the Lord looked down from up on high
To see if any would draw nigh
There was no one to intervene
So He sent His son the Nazarene

The Redeemer will come and set things straight
Those who repent will change their fate
The Spirit will come and dwell in their heart
From His Word they will not depart

But to those who reject Him He will repay
Like a pent up flood they will be swept away
He's dressed for battle and wrapped in zeal
The wrath of God He will unseal

He is the King of Kings and Lord of Lords
Out of His mouth comes a mighty sword
His reign on earth will be without end
He is my Counselor, Savior and Friend

March 8, 2017

Isaiah 59
Revelation 5:1-5
Revelation 19:11-16
Isaiah 9:1-7

Make Straight the Path

Make straight the path for the way of the Lord
His coming is certain as foretold in His Word
Proclaim far away this message in song and dance
Let stringed instruments and swirling skirts display exuberance

Prepare; prepare for the time draws near
When the harvest will be over and all will live in fear
Seals will be opened and the four horses set free
Sin's penalty will be paid by heaven's set decree

The riders will go forth on a mission to destroy
Nature will mourn seeing the weapons deploy
Famine and plague will pursue both man and beast
While carnivorous animals dine on the feast

The Lord will crush kings on the day of His great wrath
Heaping up the dead in a terrible blood bath
For the inhabitants of the land have rejected the law of the Lord
Therefore, out of Jesus' mouth will come a mighty sword

The armies of heaven will follow Him in white
Riding on white horses they join Him in the fight
Let the saints rejoice with swords in their hands
To carry out the sentence as the law demands

This is the glory of all His mighty saints
If they but believe His Word and choose not to faint
Proclaim far away this message in song and dance
Let stringed instruments and swirling skirts display exuberance

March 23, 2017

Isaiah 40:3-5 – "A voice of one calling: "In the wilderness prepare the way for the LORD; make straight in the desert a highway for our God. ⁴ Every valley shall be raised up, every mountain and hill made low; the rough ground shall become level, the rugged places a plain. ⁵ And the glory of the LORD will be revealed, and all people will see it together. For the mouth of the LORD has spoken.""

Psalm 149   Isaiah 34:1-8
Revelation 6:1-8   Revelation 19:11-19

Psalm 110:5-6   Hebrews 12:1-3
Isaiah 5:18-30   Jeremiah 31:1-14

God's Kingdom Is Coming

Storm clouds are roiling, can you not see?
Strong gale force winds blowing over the seas
They enter the coastlands of each nation
Affecting the people in every station

The Lord sees from heaven with tears in His eyes
As darkness enfolds those who believe the lies
Trouble is brewing of their own making
Consequences of sin brings a terrible shaking

Look as the earth does buckle and move
The waves do roar they cannot be soothed
For rebellion is rooted in the dust of the earth
Denying their Creator who gave them birth

But, look, in the east a light does arise
A Son breaking forth, glory filling the skies
A remnant arises to catch the Son's rays
Glory now fills them, holy fire sets them ablaze

Grace that is greater and mercy so deep
Is poured out on those who repent and weep
God's kingdom is coming, "The Day of the Lord"
It is a time of pestilence, famine and sword

Our Lord will come and vanquish His foes
And send them to eternity with unspeakable woes
He will set up His throne to reign on the earth
The nations will then gather and proclaim His worth

Get ready get ready to meet Him on high
Our Bridegroom will wait for us up in the sky
A spotless pure bride He is coming to claim
Together, forever, our love to proclaim

May 30, 2014

Isaiah 60:1-3
Matthew 24
1 Thessalonians 4:15-18
Malachi 4:1-2

The Lord's return is a topic I have been studying for decades. As the day of the Lord draws closer, we will have to draw closer to Him. That is the only way to escape the coming darkness. It is by staying in His presence we will become the pure and spotless bride we wish to be. He promised He will always be with us, even to the end of the age. We forget He sees everything we do and knows all our thoughts. How different would we live if we remembered this and welcomed Him into our daily lives, talking over all the things that happen every day? He longs for us to open the door of our heart so He can come in and fellowship with us.

There is a connection between the shaking of the earth's foundations (earthquakes) and the rebellion of the "dust of the earth" (humanity). Man was created by God to have dominion over the earth under the authority of their Creator. When man denies that connection of the One who gave them life the earth rebels under that dominion.

Prayer: Forgive us, Lord, for our rebellion of You and Your ways. Thank You for Your grace and mercy that You pour out on those who repent. We look for Your coming and wait for Your glory to be poured out on us so that we can bring Your light to a lost and dying world.

Jerusalem My Joy

Jerusalem, Jerusalem city on a hill
The joy of My inheritance to My son, Israel
You were promised this land forever and a day
No one can remove you without My final say

The nations may threaten and even bring fear
But know that heaven's army is ready and near
I will make Jerusalem an immovable rock
All who try to break it will be in for a shock

I will restore the fortunes of Israel My son
The deserts will bloom, the tribes will be one
My favor will rest upon those in the land
They will know these blessings all come from My hand

One day the Lord will return amongst songs of joy
To the temple on the hill where the priests all employ
All nations will stream to the house of God one day
The King will be crowned with His glory on display

December 27, 2016

Isaiah 62
Zechariah 12:1-5
Ezekiel 37:15-28
Isaiah 52:8-10
Psalm 45:1-7
Zechariah 8

Jesus's second coming is a "day" of darkness that will cover the earth. However, it will also be a "day" when the glory of God will rise in His people and nations will be drawn to that light. (Isaiah 60) The days leading up to the return of Christ will be a time of unprecedented harvest into the kingdom of God. Will you be ready for Christ's return?

For those who have ever wondered about the second return of Christ or questioned how to be prepared, this insightful guide uses the truths of Scripture to answer questions such as:

o What is the rapture?
o Will all Christians be taken in the rapture?
o How is Jesus' return like the "days of Noah"?
o How is the rapture a picture of the ancient Jewish wedding customs?

Author Debbie Furey has spent countless hours in prayer and study uncovering hidden prophecies throughout the Bible related to Jesus Christ's second coming. One such prophecy in the book of Ruth paints a picture of the return of the Jews coming back into their land shortly before the marriage of Jesus Christ and His church. Another prophecy is hidden in the Song of Solomon - the parable of the five wide and five foolish virgins of Matthew 25, which explains what will happen to those who are ready and those who are not.

Read about all this and more in her book: "The Rapture: Behold the Bridegroom Cometh!"

For more information visit: www.debbiefureysbooks.com

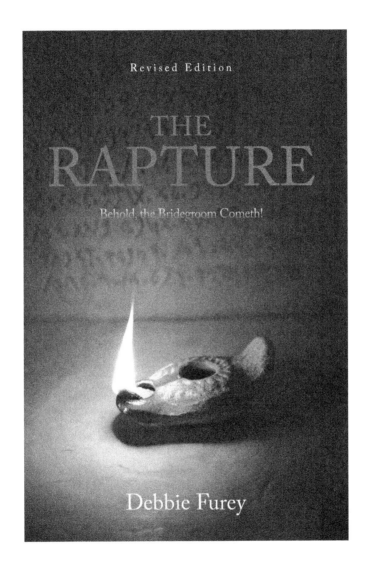

SIA information can be obtained
ww.ICGtesting.com
d in the USA
1s0431230917
3BV00005B/7/P

9 781947 491151